MOHAMMED THE PROPHET
The Perfect Man - The Complete Man

Imam W. Deen Mohammed®

بسم الله الرحمن الرحيم

بسم الله الرحمن الرحيم

CONTENTS

بسم الله الرحمن الرحيم

Imam W. Deen Mohammed, leader of the largest community of Muslims in the United States of America passed on September 9, 2008. We pray that his work continues to grow and serve humanity as he would have desired it to, through all of us who have benefited so greatly from his teachings. Ameen

Structure, Guard and Publish the Knowledge

"We need knowledge, then we need protection for it. How do you protect knowledge? Some people say, "You protect knowledge by not letting anybody interfere with it. Don't let anybody change it. Publish it! When you publish it, people know it. That's its protection." Yes! If you want to protect your knowledge, publish it! When you publish it, it is protected and the people know it. But if you keep it locked up to yourself, you will die and your knowledge will die with you. Or your enemy will get a hold to it and he will publish it after you in a corrupt form.

Thus, Allah (swt) says. "And We have revealed it for the express purpose that it should be propagated." Yes! That is its guarantee that it will be protected. When it's propagated in its right form, then the people will inherit it directly. They don't have to listen to what you have to say. You won't have to tell them what Prophet Mohammed ﷺ said, they got it directly. It was published by him in his lifetime.

If we want to guard the knowledge that we have, we must publish it. The more people know about it, the more it is guaranteed that it will live and it won't be changed. The less people know about it, the better the chance that it will die with us, or be changed. Yes! We structure the knowledge and we propagate the knowledge." *Imam W. Deen Mohammed*

V

Abbreviations Clarified

G-d for G-d
In this book the word G-d is written as G-d for the respect of the word "G-d" because some people mirror to disrespect it with the word "dog".

SWT for Subhana Wa Tallah
The abbreviation after Allah (SWT) means "Subhana Wa Tallah" in Arabic which means "The Sacred and The Mighty" in English.

ﷺ / PBUH for Peace Be Upon Him

The abbreviation after Prophet Mohammed ﷺ or (PBUH) means "May the Peace and Blessings of Allah (G-d) be upon him" in English and "Sal Allahu Allahi Wa Salam" in Arabic.

AS for Alayhi Salam
The abbreviation (AS) means "Alayhi Salam" in Arabic, which means "May Allah (G-d) bless him" in English.

بسم الله الرحمن الرحيم

MOHAMMED: THE PROPHET ﷺ
The Perfect Man – The Complete Man

Mohammed: The Prophet ﷺ

Believers, we glorify G-d, we worship none but him. We put our faith in him. We trust him. We do not separate from belief and we witness that Mohammed ﷺ is the servant and messenger of G-d and the last of the Prophets; the seal of the Prophets mentioned in the Qur'an as the one, also mentioned in the Torah and in the Gospel, the Injil, as one who comes to purify the people and to relieve them of the yokes of slavery – the burdens that bend their backs down.

This Prophet Mohammed ﷺ is given to us by G-d in the Qur'an as a mercy to all the worlds. He is a mercy to all the worlds and he's also given to us, by G-d in the Qur'an, as the most excellent model for human beings to have as a model of what the human being should be under G-d or for his creator; most excellent model. Not just for Muslims, he's an excellent model for any who believe in G-d and believe in the last day.

See, this Prophet is given to the whole world, not just to Muslims. We know everyone is created to be Muslim, but the conscious Muslims are only those who follow the guidance of G-d in the Qur'an and as Mohammed the Prophet ﷺ, demonstrated how the Qur'an should be followed. So we follow the Qur'an, the word of G-d, as Mohammed the Prophet ﷺ, demonstrated that to us – then we are Muslims in the proper sense. Again, I want to repeat that Mohammed ﷺ is not only a model leader for those who know of themselves to be Muslims, Mohammed ﷺ is a model leader for any people who are sincere; believing in G-d and believing in judgment day, a day when they have to account to G-d, before G-d, for their life – how they lived their life in this world. So Mohammed ﷺ is a mercy to all the worlds and the Qur'an itself is the mercy and Mohammed ﷺ delivered the Qur'an to the worlds and he and his model human constitution, is a mercy to all the worlds. His mercy is the message that He gives and the life that He lives – the human life. The message and the human life are both a mercy to us.

When I began to be seriously interested in the life of Mohammed the Prophet ﷺ, I read books but then I began to study him myself on my own. I studied him in the Qur'an (what G-d says of him), I studied him in the context of revelation, in the history of revelation, how it unfolds, and I came to see that he is really, the product, the finished product, of the human being. G-d began making the human being with Adam. He made the natural man and then Mohammed ﷺ was presented to us as the finished product. Now here is the complete man. This is the complete man and I believe in the Islamic studies; the learned people refer to him as that, the complete man, the perfect man, he's both!

The perfect man and the complete man and this Prophet is a teacher – he's an educator and the miracle is that he himself was not educated. There were no schools in Saudi Arabia. It was an undeveloped place as far as enlightenment was concerned and there were no colleges, no universities for him to attend. He's an uneducated man and he is selected by G-d because of his model excellence. He was having that model excellence before G-d made him a messenger to the world or to the believers. He was already a model man. G-d says "that he has already lived a lifetime among you".

He's already lived a lifetime among you and the people
who knew him – the pagans, the idolaters and even the
Hanafi people (those who did not worship idols), a few of
them, companions of the Prophet ﷺ and a few others,
they all knew him before he received the message of G-d,
called to be the Prophet, a messenger. They knew him to
be a man that was having (uswatan hasanah). So he had
this (uswatan hasanah – most beautiful character) before
he was called to be messenger and to me it was very
logical that G-d would not call those who were leaning
over to the left or the right, or falling on their faces, but he
would call the man who was level headed and upright to
be his messenger; his mercy to all the worlds.

On this point I would like to say that we should look to
Mohammed the Prophet ﷺ, and to the leadership that he
formed as the messenger of G-d, as a mercy to all the
worlds, to see how we should form our leadership today.
And we find that Mohammed the Prophet ﷺ, selected
from different nationalities and they were in his company.
They were in his group, his special group of leaders, to

reach the others. So we are living now in a country, brothers – America. And this is a multinational country, multiethnic country, pluralistic country, and Muslims are here now from the different colors of man and from the different nationalities and cultural backgrounds, etc.

I had suggested for us, and I think this is your suggestion, too, that no matter how small our leadership group is (for example, my ministry) I call it W. Deen Mohammed's Ministry, and I did that because I wanted to be free from having any obligations to any other organization, so I formed my own ministry.

I didn't want to have people holding me back on interfering with the direction that I saw for Muslims. So rather than join people where I have to argue and have problems, I formed my own ministry and yet work with other people! And I want to work with other people. So I formed my own ministry and my ministry now does not have a white person in it, but Insha'Allah, I'm looking for that European American, I'm looking for that white person. I want a white person in it and, Insha'Allah, I will have it; African and white, European and I will have an

Arab and I'll have Indians. I want it to be colorful. I want it to represent people – humanity. And I think we should try to do this as much as possible; even the business organizations that we have. If you're going to do big business, then have Muslims of different nationalities working with you. And this is not only the way for Islam to go; this is the way the world is going. The world is going like that and it's time for Islam to step out ahead of the world because Islam is the leader of the world. The world is not the leader of Islam.

Our Prophet, if we study his way, we will see that today the world is shaping to receive Mohammed's ﷺ way. It's becoming a world that's thinking of itself as one community, a world community, all people belonging to one community. The system is beginning to respect the oneness of human family. We are the people that should be in front of this. We are Muslims. We were told by G-d "that the people are one people. Mankind was created to be one community" and we see now that the world is waking up; that mankind is one global community and economics, politics and everything is being affected now by that reality – that mankind is intended to be one community.

The Prophet ﷺ in Medina, he was able to establish the community; the first community of Islam – the Ummah. He was able to establish that community by the grace of G-d to him, as the mercy to all people. He was able to establish that community and that community should now be our pattern, model for our direction. Mohammed, the Prophet ﷺ was the leader leading people in all healthy constructs of social, societal community life; in all healthy constructs. Whatever is halal, we should embrace it. Whatever the community needs, the community of man needs, the Muslim leadership should be seeking ways to provide that and to, at least, provide the guidance for that.

So we can't be secular Muslims and we can't be spiritual Muslims without the whole life. We want to be Muslims, whole Muslims, complete Muslims. To be complete Muslims we have to look at community; that's where we are to go. G-d wants us to focus on community. G-d says of us – "if we're the best and most useful." It not only means the best in the moral sense, or the best in spiritual sense, it means the best in practical sense. We're the best also in the practical sense. G-d says, "and who has said to his servants, his devotees that such and such of the goods that G-d provides is forbidden to them" say, "so these are from him and even more. In the hereafter, it should be exclusively for them" al-hamdu-lillah! Allahu-Akbar! Allahu-Akbar! How wonderful G-d is, how glorious G-d is.

How wonderful G-d is and how wonderfully and miraculously he has guided the Ummah of Mohammed ﷺ, Ummah of the Muslims. So let us be thoughtful of these things and all of us join our best leaders and focus on community. We no more should be just satisfied with building our own selves up as pious people; pious people doing dhikrs and salat because if that's all we have to offer is dhiker's and salats, G-d will say to us in the judgment what Mohammed ﷺ said to those who had that to offer.

He said, "Is that all they do? Well who takes care of them? Who provides their food? Who provides their clothing? Who provides shelter for them? Well, those people are better than they, better than those who just do dhikr and salat and fast and live a life of the pious people."

Piety is really doing your job in community life and community begins with our families. Let us be men responsible for our household and let us be men loving to do work that brings in a lawful income. The Muslim, if he understands his religion, his religion makes him love work and love to perfect things, to make things excellent.

Mohammed, the Prophet ﷺ said, "A believer is the one who, when he does a thing, he seeks to perfect it. He seeks to make it perfect". He wants to make it as best as he possibly can and this is the best spirit in a human being. We see for little children; some of them don't care about perfecting their work, but we'll notice one little child wants to do everything correct; not satisfied until it looks perfect and beautiful. That's the Islam, that's the spirit of Muslim that G-d put in him and is manifesting in him.

Dear brothers, we also should look at something else. Islam is for the generations to inherit and this inheritance began with Mohammed's ﷺ Ummah. So aren't we the inheritors? If we're truly his followers, of the Ummah of Mohammed ﷺ, if we're the inheritors of that, we don't want to see it put back just as it was then. We want to see it put back better than it was then, and this is something that we have to shake ourselves and wake up to – that we're not just to match what was done in the past.

We're supposed to contribute to the work that was done in the past so that it is greater, bigger, more beneficial, more useful, for all the good people. Don't look and say they had so many camels, and they had so much wealth, and they did this with this wealth. Look at the world today and see how much we need to get, to step out ahead of this world. We should be in front of this world. That's my spirit and I love it! So we should devote ourselves to establishment. And we know that the Prophet ﷺ was one to purify us. We're not going anywhere to be successful unless we accept to fight indecency in our lives. Fight bad morals! Fight ignorance. Fight selfishness. We have to refine ourselves. We have to take charge of ourselves.

The Muslim is one who's told that he should take responsibility for himself and then accept a share of the responsibility for the whole society. And unless we do this we're not completing our job as Muslims. Accept responsibility for ourselves, our family and then for the whole society. We have to accept a share in the responsibility for the good state and the good future of the whole society.

And we know also that the Muslim should be in the forefront of education. I know we're behind, colonial domination kept putting us all behind. We're behind, but while we're trying to catch up, we should realize that our aim should not just be to catch up. Our aim should be to take the lead. And we have a few Muslims in the Islamic world who think this way. I know. I've met them. They think this way and it's just a matter of time before the Muslim intellect and morality is going to be leading the whole world of civilized society. It's just a matter of time!

I call this the day of religion, not the day of judgment. I call this the day of religion. I know what's shaping up in the world because I'm busy mixing with the leaders. They call themselves the actors and the players and I say to myself silently, G-d says, "we did not create this world for sport and play. So you take this world for sport and play, but we were not playing when we created this world." So when they called themselves actors and players I recall what G-d says, "that we were not playing when we created this great universe".

So let us be very serious brothers and let us not be so stiff in our own opinions and so stiff in our own form, cultural form, that we can't see the bigger picture. The bigger picture is not our opinions, the bigger picture is not how we are formed culturally. The bigger picture is the guidance of G-d for all of us and Mohammed ﷺ as the model leader for all people who believe in G-d and the last day. As-Salaamu-Alaikum

Prophet Mohammed ﷺ

We glorify G-d; we witness that he is one! We know that he created us for his service. G-d said that he neither created men nor jinn except to be his servants. And I have talked with Christian preachers and ministers and the deacons in the churches and I hear them speak with pride. Sometimes they say they would rather be a servant at the door, a doorman in the kingdom of heaven than to have the best job in this world. Now I don't know if they practice that or not, but that is what they said to me.

I know that if we understand that Allah has made all of us, created all of us to be his servants. Mohammed ﷺ is the servant par excellence, but we are also servants of G-d; ya'ebaadullah. That's how G-d refers to us, all people as ya'ebaad, especially men, as ya'ebaadullah. Oh, servants of G-d, oh workers for G-d! And G-d says, "And surely I'm a worker and I'm working in my place. Work also in your places". So this is not a call for people who want to be idle, or want to be lazy, or want to give up their responsibility. This is a call for those who want to accept their responsibility and want to make a contribution to the betterment of the whole human society. We pray to G-d and glorify him. We ask him to strengthen us in our faith.

We ask him to strengthen our faith and make us strong for Islam.

Our Lord, give us good in this world and good in the hereafter and save us from the fires of sin. Now look what G-d has said. G-d says that, "my mercy extends to all," and then he comes behind and says, "now I should ordain it for those who do right and practice regular charity and who believe in our signs." It means who believe in the religion, right, who believe in religion – all of it! You see what has come from G-d? So what is this saying to us? It is saying that, yes, the people that you think need punishment (perhaps they do need punishment) but if you keep on doing my job, a lot of these people that are earning punishment now, they're going to see, in time, and they're going to be affected. They're going to repent and they're going to start doing right and practicing charity and believing in our signs. So look, if I carry out your wishes right now Moses, we won't have any people for the future.

Praise be to Allah, so let's continue now. Now, look how G-d is going to bring these people, (because after all, who did he have among those people except Moses)? Even

Aaron turned backwards. So who did G-d have among them except Moses? He had nobody but Moses. But the people that he was going to make were going to come from that very people; oh yes! Let's continue this reading now. He ordained it for them. It goes on to describe them, "those who follow the apostle." So that's a guarantee from Allah! "I know the state of these people now, Moses. But you're going to have followers from these people – those who follow the apostle, the unlettered Prophet." Now a lot of us don't know that Moses was an unlettered Prophet. But now Allah is speaking through Moses at what Prophet Mohammed ﷺ would be, at his situation.

The situation he would face and how he would triumph, too. And the man is in the same condition as Moses was in; a man who's uneducated. Moses said, "Oh, G-d, I fear to go before Pharaoh and his priests or his magicians" why? Because they were very clever - they were very articulate. They were high people. They were the high and mighty. So Moses said, "G-d, this is too much for me?" He said, "Would you untie the knot in my tongue?" What does it mean? Would you give me the speech that they have! Would you give me the ability to articulate, to speak clearly, to speak very persuasively, to command the language, will you give me command of the language, command of the tongue that they have? Then I won't feel so embarrassed going before them, G-d. G-d said, "That's going to take a little time, Moses. He said, well, then will you help Aaron out so he can see what we have to do. Aaron is a pretty smooth talker. Now you can just show him where, what we have to do here, G-d. Make him a helper for me. G-d said, ok, don't worry about it; that much we can do right now. Ok, you got Aaron. Aaron will go with you and he will be a speaker for you.

Those who follow the apostle, the unlettered Prophet, the uneducated Prophet, whom they find mentioned in their own scriptures – in the law and the Gospel – that means the Old Testament, the Torah and the Gospel, the New Testament. For he commands them what is just and forbids them what is evil. That's the distinguishing mark. If he is the right one, if he is the liberator – we're talking about liberator. If he is the liberator that's coming, his distinguishing mark is that he stands upon what is right. He stands against wrong and he stands up for right. That's his distinguishing mark. He allows them as lawful what is good and pure, and he prohibits them from what is bad and impure. That's his mark.

We got people who say they are leaders. They want us to recognize them. Church leaders, other leaders, TV made leaders and they want us to recognize them as being the proper leader for all of us. "Oh, yeah, he is the proper leader, that's the one with the credentials!" But is he standing up for right and standing against wrong? But that's not all. See the test gets harder. Is he encouraging the people; putting a sanction on what is good and pure and holding them back from what is bad and impure.   In other words, we can't have leaders that get out there and say, "Oh, I'm for you man, and we got to have so many jobs, or we got to have this civil rights bill passed. But you don't see my brother who's a wine head, who's got a good mind, but he's given himself to the influences of this neighborhood and he's lying in the gutter. You don't see the crime building who up in my neighborhood. You don't see the black crime spreading all over the community. You don't see the bad eating habits of the people that are cutting off their life. That's giving them high blood pressure, that's raising the incidence of cancer in their life.

You don't see all of this. You don't see pork affecting
them. You don't see whiskey affecting them. You don't
see dope bothering them. You aren't addressing these
problems. You're just talking about jobs and civil rights.
You don't meet the qualification of the liberator in this
verse.

How to liberate people? This is the way you liberate them!
He releases them from the heavy burdens and from the
yokes. What are the yokes? Sin! Immorality! Vulgar
behavior! Don't you know that's what got us enslaved?
Why don't we have the strength and the dignity of other
communities? It's because we have given ourselves to this
kind of deterioration and our leaders won't stand up and
say that's wrong. This is part of your problem. We're
going to have to have better morals among the blacks.
They won't do that. You release them from the heavy
burdens, from the yokes that are upon them. So it is those
who believe in him and honor him and help him and
follow the light which is sent down with him. It is they
who will be successful. Isn't that wonderful? There is no
question in our minds. If we're not successful, we only

have to look at this one verse. We'll see why we're not successful.

Say "o men! I am sent unto you all as the apostle of Allah; that is the apostle of the one G-d, the one and only G-d to whom belongs (he's going to make it clear so there's no doubt in your mind at all), the dominion of the skies and the earth." Say, "Who is this Allah you're talking about"? The one who owns whatever you see up there and whatever is down here – is that clear? There is no G-d but He. It is He that giveth both life and death. So believe in Allah and his apostle, the unlettered Prophet who believes in Allah. He believes in Allah and in his word. Therefore, follow him that you may be guided right. This is the Qur'an! Alright, so here you see the picture of the liberator; the promised liberator. The Christians call him the savior and they have made him Jesus Christ, the promised liberator who will come and he will not compromise with wrong. He will do what he has to do and that's it. And he will free the people, not only for some of the yoke, from some of the burdens, but from all of it. He will not be one to speak hard on this problem, and be mum on another problem because he doesn't want to get into too much trouble, don't want to rock the boat. He won't be that kind of leader, praise be to Allah.

Now how are we to understand that difference between Jesus and Prophet Mohammed (peace be upon them)? Now we know Jesus, according to scripture, he came among the people and he did the same thing. What he saw that was wrong he spoke out against it and he seemed like he was occupied with the needs of the oppressed, the poor.

Some of you perhaps are aware of the Good Samaritan. The story of the Good Samaritan and how Jesus condemned those who passed by the suffering person in the road. The poor and neglected person –a bum in the road and he needed health care, he needed guidance, he needed friends; a friend in society. And Jesus, he condemned them; those who were charged with helping him (in the religion – the Rabbi's, the doctors of law). Instead of them doing something about it, they walked around him, crossed on the other side of the street so they wouldn't even be disturbed by him. So we know Jesus was a person who had that sensitivity, so how are we to understand the two people – the two great figures – Jesus,

the Prophet and Mohammed the Prophet (peace be upon
them).

Here is the way we understand them. Now, there are many
ways, but here is one great way to understand the two and
their differences. Jesus, he came to revive the moral
sensitivities and in reviving the moral sensitivities, then
this would be help for the people who were suffering
injustices. Right? So that's how he came. He's called a
friend. He's called a doctor. He's called many things.
That's how he comes. Now he didn't come to educate.
How do we know? Because when Jesus sent his disciples
out, he said, "don't write down anything, take no thought
as to what you will say. Just go there and when you get
there, the spirit will move you." And he's called what? The
son of the Holy Spirit! Is that not right? He's called the son
or the child of the Holy Spirit. That's Jesus, son of Mary in
the Qur'an, but in the Gospel, son of the Holy Spirit. To
let us know that that was typical of him is the spiritual
man. You see, he was born of the Holy Spirit.

He's the spiritual man and we know that he was a rational
Prophet. He was perfectly rational because he argued with

them in a very logical way, and condemned them and their behavior on the strength of what was in the law and in the prophecy. So it's not to say he wasn't logical, he was logical, he was rational but he was not the teacher of rational discourse. He came to quicken life, "and the first Adam, he was the living soul and the second Adam, Jesus in symbolic terminology, is what, quickening spirit. And in the last book of the Bible, in revelations, how does it close out, "I come quick." Isn't that what it says?

Well it's talking about Jesus; Jesus, but not that Jesus, it's talking about spirit that Jesus was typical of. Jesus was born of the spirit and his life and mission is typical of the spirit and the same spirit will come again. And when it comes again, it will quicken life again, you see. That's what its saying. So Jesus, in the beginning of the Gospel, he is the son, born of the spirit and the son of the spirit and then, in the end of the book, the angels of Jesus come through the revelators, John the revelator – and he tells John, the revelator many things; leads him into many wonders, gave him insight into many wonders. And then John, the revelator, he ends it, says don't touch this, don't take anything away from this, don't add any more to this that has been revealed behold, I come quick - means don't apply your rational mind.

Here is John, the revelator telling them this same thing but many can't see it. He's telling them don't apply your rational mind to this, the spirit has brought this on. This has come by inspiration and the way of this order is not to put it to logical scrutiny; subjected to logical scrutiny or try to improve upon it rationally. That's not the way of this order. The way of this order is to wait until the Holy Spirit hits another.

Alright, I'm sure you understand, but there's another order that has to come in. What is that? The spirit of truth, says, "When he has come, he will lead you into all truth." It didn't say you have to wait on the spirit. It won't come quick, and Allah says in the Qur'an, "in this Qur'an it's sent down in gradual measures." Not quick, in gradual measures. It's an educating process. There's a difference. These two complement each other and one must come before the other. How can people follow a good line of reasoning and they can't follow a good line of feeling? You don't know how to feel right about people, how are you going to think right about people. You can't feel right in a given situation, how are you going to think right in that given situation? So, the first thing is for G-d to bring about a condition to make people sensitive, to what's right, so they will feel right, and after they can feel right, then you can show them how to think right. So Jesus is a necessary, he's a necessary condition before Mohammed ﷺ. Jesus must come first, then Mohammed ﷺ. Praise be to Allah! Now, dear beloved people, Prophet Mohammed ﷺ is the educator from among the illiterate. A lot of us don't know that Jesus, too, was not schooled.

His mother was a holy woman and she grew up in a holy religious order. Jesus was born to her out of that order. Then Jesus didn't come under the teachings of that order. Jesus came into his mission and his teachings by inspiration; the Holy Spirit and he surprised them and amazed them when he encountered them. They were so amazed at his insight. He wasn't taught; he wasn't educated. G-d had inspired him to have that kind of insight and he surpassed them and he became their leader, their master, according to the words of the scripture. So we have to understand that. But here, one must come behind him, and Jesus said "look I must go away, it's expedient that I go away", meaning that it's a necessity of G-d's law that I go away, for if I go not away, the comforter will not come unto you.

You see how important it is for us to know how G-d caused great, major changes to take place in the intellect of the people in order to bring them out of slavery (mental slavery) into life. He has to first make them morally sensitive, then after making them morally sensitive, then they are agreeable to be educated. Who are the hardest people to educate; it's the sinful people – those who are prone to doing wrong. They're the hardest one's to talk sense to. This is very important that we know this because, look, if I'm an individual that wants to improve my intellect, if I accept this as being a profound fact of my behavioral nature; that your brain just doesn't work right when your spirit is given to wrong doing, then, if I want my brain to be more excellent, I'll try to bring my spirit to conform to better moral life. Oh, yes, and that's the key.

Look at this western society. This is important, believe me this is very important – especially for us. I remember as a child, ten years old, when this country, the majority of white people in this country, took pride in themselves as people who believed in refined morals. But look what has happened over the last twenty years. Now, the majority of white people they're just as lost or wasted, as the people who they used to call uneducated negroes. Now, in this period that we're talking about, in this period of moral degeneration, that we're talking about right now, we have also seen the economic crash, or the economic deterioration of this nation. Is that not a fact? So here we're talking about what G-d says, and I'm pointing to you, I'm pointing evidence out to you that what G-d said, here's the proof of it. G-d says, "That the condition for intellectual excellence is moral excellence." There's no such thing as intellectual excellence if you don't have moral excellence – and I'm showing you a fact in history that's within your grasp! It's not before your time and we're able to see this manifest, where the moral deterioration set in and the intellect - they start talking about what? A brain drainage. Isn't that what they told us? There's a brain drainage on the country. Oh, yes, and with that also is a crumbling of business. If this in not plain, if this is not evidence, then what will convince the people that Allah's way is the right way? You won't be convinced. If this won't convince you, you'll never be convinced. So we repeat that the moral condition is necessary for the second condition. Now you say, well how does that apply to Prophet Mohammed ﷺ? The jahiliyyah, the ignorance, the corrupt age was there before Prophet Mohammed ﷺ. But Jesus was before Prophet Mohammed ﷺ too, and many people were not given to that corruption. There were still many good people – like the one who heard of Prophet Mohammed ﷺ and said, "Yes, I believe I know who he is!" Wasn't that one of those who left from Jesus? He said, "I believe I know who he is." He said, "Our scripture tells us about a man like this." They were the ones who turned to the messenger, Prophet Mohammed ﷺ, and became good Muslims.

Who gave him haven? What country gave him a rescue from the ignorance of his own people; from their violence? It was Christian Ethiopia. So you can't separate Prophet Mohammed ﷺ and Jesus. And what did Prophet

Mohammed ﷺ say? "And in the end, they shall see me and Christ Jesus together!" How are they going to be together; as necessary complements to each other? Now, the Jesus, the Christ principal, the Christ nature has to be in Prophet Mohammed ﷺ; if Prophet Mohammed ﷺ is to become Mohammed. Mohammed is the intellect that praises G-d and champions the cause of fallen humanity. But he can't become Mohammed in his body without Jesus.

What is he saying - just hold on, not that Jesus, but the Christ nature? What does Allah say of Prophet Mohammed ﷺ, "say, I have lived a lifetime among you!" Prophet Mohammed ﷺ then has two lives. He says in the Qur'an, "and I have lived a lifetime among you." What was that lifetime? Up to forty years old – up to forty years old; that was the lifetime. Now, he had lived forty years and he's told by Allah, to tell the people that I have lived a lifetime among you!" The lifetime is forty years. Now, we can't go into this fully, but Allah gave us some things that we have to digest rationally in part and the rest of it by faith. That's why I say we can't do this completely. See that cross and that forty, they are the same.

Jesus picked up the cross and he told the other people, "pick up my cross." Isn't that what he said? He said, "Pick up my cross!" So that tells us that Jesus had a cross and that cross must have been good and the world (according to the Bible, according to the Gospel), we know it is a sign, but according to the Gospel, the world crucified him on a cross. So there's a good cross and a bad cross. And I'm telling you now, that the forty and the cross are the same. So what are we talking about? We're talking about the behavioral nature that Allah put in man; the behavioral nature that Allah has given – your inborn natural behavioral nature. So, Prophet Mohammed ﷺ, without inspiration, without revelation, he had kept his cross intact. His cross was good. His cross had stood up. If you don't know this, I'm telling you right now, a cross – Jesus himself, is a cross. So they put the man as a cross and put him on the cross, but actually, the true cross is the man; he's the true cross. The false cross is the cross behind him, the one he was nailed to and the false cross is made of wood. It's made of a tree. And the Bible says, "Cursed be he that hangs in the tree!" Is that not the Bible? So what is the tree? The tree is the culture. There's religion, there's the word of G-d. The word of G-d brings light and understanding, and the people form customs after the teachings of G-d and in time you have customs or what we call culture after the teachings of G-d. Christian culture is a cross. Christian culture crucifies believers. Is that not the truth? But what does it have connections with? Does Christian culture educate? Christian culture manipulates behavior. What behavior? The forty that G-d gave you – forty is symbolic of it. Why is it forty? G-d says, "And he had given every creature his needs in four periods." And when those four essentials come into your conscience, you multiply them by ten, that's forty! So you see, they put him on a cross, but actually he's a cross. Balanced man. Proportioned man – see, the old artists, they used to stretch the man out and they put his hands and span his feet and his hands and they show that he's a balanced figure. His arms and his legs – they all go out in a balance and they can touch the circle. Put him in the center and his legs and his hands touch the circle – and his head, right? So it's typical of the balance that G-d has made in man and we know what extending the hands means helping humanity.

His hands go out in both directions to the fullest. On one side you got the uneducated people – his hand goes out to them. On the other side you got the establishment, the rulers – his hand goes out to them. One hand goes out and the other hand goes out – and the desire to help both are just as strong. Some liberators, they have a compassion for the oppressed, but they forget that the rulers are also oppressed. Their ignorance has oppressed them. Their sins have oppressed them. So both are oppressed – those who are on the top and those who are on the bottom; they both are oppressed and they both deserve a chance but here's another thing; those who can call the left may not be able to call the right. To call the left, all you need is a preacher. To call the right, you need an educator. You have to extend the charity out to both. Hayya 'alas salah! Hayya alal falah! See, on this side, they need cultivating. On this side they need educating. Praise be to Allah! See, don't forget when you're making your salat, you're reciting the words of Qur'an. That's the highest wisdom! Oh, yes, that's the education. Praise be to Allah! So, we're still talking about the liberator here. Now, Prophet Mohammed ﷺ, I'm telling you with authority of Qur'an, with insight into Qur'an, nobody told me this. The Qur'an tells me this, and that's the best authority. I'm telling you, from my study of Qur'an, and the Sunnah of Prophet Mohammed ﷺ, the life of Prophet Mohammed ﷺ that the forty years that he said, "I have lived a lifetime among you." He was telling them that, "I have fulfilled the sign in Jesus."

What is the sign in Jesus – that this life comes without teachers; comes without Prophethood. How do we know? Because Jesus spoke while he was in the cradle; he wasn't a Prophet yet. According to the Gospel, he became a Prophet when he was a man and the dove lit down upon his shoulder – that was the sign that he was G-d's Prophet; that the mission had come to him. When he was a baby, it had already been predicted that he would be the one, but it hadn't come to him yet. But the Qur'an said, "He spoke even while he was in the cradle." And the Bible says, "As a young man, he went into the synagogue and he spoke and he just astounded the people." His knowledge was so great, his insight so great, that he just amazed the teachers in the synagogue but was he a Prophet yet? No, not according to the book; he was not a Prophet yet. How did he get this great insight? Because of his nature; the nature

was right. The spirit was right. The influence was right. He
was born of Mary. His environmental influence was good
and right and perfect and he had grown up, he had
developed out of that perfect environment. So his behavior
was right. His heart was right. His appetite was right his
feelings were right, so he lived the highest life – morally
speaking. And of Prophet Mohammed ﷺ, Allah said,

"And we have seen him, that he is on the highest plane of
moral excellence". This is before he became the Prophet
ﷺ. And we have beheld him. We beheld him on the
highest plane of moral excellence – and that's what the
history tells us, that Prophet Mohammed ﷺ, though he
lived around all that ignorance and corruption, he never
became a victim of it. He was always a man of high
morals. They called him El-Amin, the honest and
trustworthy one, even before he was the Prophet ﷺ,
that's what they called him. He was not vulgar, he was not
indecent. He was not unjust and when he went to the
mountain to seek seclusion away from the people, hoping
that he would find some way there, meditate and find some
way to just correct the problems. What was moving him?
What was the urge that was driving him in the mountain?

It was the burden of the people. History tells us that Prophet Mohammed ﷺ was so burdened because of the ignorance and sins and human abuses that was going on in the world that he took refuge from that kind of condition, situation into the mountain and there he sat in solitude and cried out, poured out his heart to G-d not knowing where to find G-d. He was just wondering in his eyes and in his mind, G-d oh, G-d, wherever you are…. understand another thing – that is Jesus' life, before he became a Prophet (which he didn't become a Prophet like Prophet Mohammed ﷺ, he became a different kind of Prophet.

But in his life before he became a Prophet there are signs to tell us something; says he was born in a manger and he was born among animals. What does that tells you – that his birth was natural behavior. The animal is natural behavior. I don't think I need to say much more. And Prophet Mohammed ﷺ – who had taught him? Nobody!

Why was his behavior so good? Natural behavior! So, Allah is telling us that even among the worst conditions, natural behavior can triumph and you can have the excellence of behavior even in a bad situation. Jesus was favored with a good situation, wasn't he, but his mother wasn't because they wouldn't even receive her in the nice hotels (according to the Bible). Say, the inns were closed against her and she had to have her baby in an animal stall, a manger. Is that not right? So what is that telling us? That is telling us that the poor masses, the world rejected us, they looked down on us. They don't consider us fit to come in their society. So they excluded us from their society. So we don't have a chance to benefit from the environmental conditions that they benefit from; the learning environment; the moral – high moral environment. We don't have a chance to benefit from that and if we want to raise our children, we're not favored with that kind of situation. Our children have to be raised up in the worst circumstances, among the worst people, in the worst circumstances, but Mary, blessed Mary, she was a perfect, good woman, pure woman and even in those circumstances she wasn't affected. She was still loyal and devoted to G-d. So her child, because of her influence comes out like her. But now, when he comes out from her, where does he find himself? Among thieves and robbers, cut throats, wine heads, drunkards. You see, Jesus was only in such an environment as long as he was with his mother, but when he was born (see delivered means put out from the mother) where did they find him – in a manger with animals! Here is the environment; here is the situation that she has to raise her child in – where animals are. But if you understand the nativity, the picture of nativity, the animals that are there are harmless animals which tells us that the Mary's influence was so strong that she had attracted harmless animals; those bad, vicious animals they didn't care for Mary, they're far away. They didn't want to live around Mary's house. They didn't find anything there that they liked but all the little nice animals were there around Mary. What does it mean? It means that the people had no education, that's all. All these signs are pointing to the absence of education. They had no education. They had nothing to depend on but the nature G-d gave them. And because of them having the fear of G-d in them and sticking to the way of G-d, then G-d blessed that nature with inspiration – divine inspiration! And when it first comes, it doesn't come to Jesus directly, it comes to Mary. Says, "And the Holy Ghost overpowered Mary and she became pregnant with a child of the Holy Ghost. Is that not right? No intellect yet; the process of the intellect is not going yet. This is the spirit; and she became pregnant with a child of the Holy Ghost." Then that child came out with a will and desire. A spirit to obey G-d.

Imam W. Deen Mohammed

Come out among animals and grow up and confound the wise with his tongue. Say, "Where did you get that from, who taught you?" The flesh is right; the spirit has come into it. I see by the inspiration of G-d.

Before he gets forty (according to scripture, they crucified him). He wasn't forty. What would have happened if he had lived to see forty? If he had lived to see forty, he would have died to Jesus and become Mohammed ﷺ, but it wasn't meant for that to happen then. But, never the less, he was a sign that it would happen. It's much to talk about. This is a big subject. The hour he was crucified is important. Say, "And they crucified him in the ninth hour." That's the hour we are on Arafat. Say, "They crucified him in the ninth hour." And in the eleventh hour he died. Right? They crucified him in the ninth hour, and in the eleventh hour he died.

We need what the others have got and believe me, this is what they've got that they didn't give us, ok? Look at the word eleven. E- L- E- V- E- N! VEN is something! VEN means what? Intellect, urge in the intellect. It's that cognitive urge. It's not knowledge; it's the urge in the intellect. It wants to know. So the last part of it refers to that urge in the intellect, to know. And the first part of it refers to high levels E-L. The EL that you catch, it's up and above the ground sound.

So in the eleventh hour he died. What is this talking about? What is the ninth hour? Why was he crucified in the ninth hour? He was crucified in the ninth hour because the world didn't want him and his mission was to come into the world, but the world didn't want him. The world is nine. You see, nine represents the world and since the world didn't want him the world crucified him. Crucifying him in the ninth hour means crucifying him in the world. In other words, they make Jesus, the moral mission of Jesus, dead in the world. But now he isn't dead, he's just dead in the world in the ninth hour. Then comes the tenth hour and he must have died in the tenth hour or maybe he didn't, we don't know, but I believe he died quite a bit in the tenth hour; maybe he didn't die out, but I think he died quite a bit in the tenth hour, too. But we know for sure that he died (according to the scripture, the Gospel, the Christian report) in the eleventh hour. So what is this talking about?

The ninth hour is the world. The tenth hour is conscience. The eleventh hour is reasoning; the ability to reason. The scholarly plain is the eleventh hour, you see. That's the scholarly plain. So it says that in the eleventh hour he died; why did he have to die in the eleventh hour? He has to die there because he represents the spirit, the impulse, and impulse must die in order for logic to work. You can't figure out the logical order of things following the impulse. The impulse just takes you up to that door, then you have to stop following impulse. You have to follow the vein of logic. That's the eleventh hour. Now you know the church begins in the eleventh hour, doesn't it? So that tells you that the church is supposed to be educating, but instead of educating, they just elevate. The real elevation is knowledge. Moses went up into the mountains for what? Knowledge! The wise man in Kenya, what sent him up into the Kenyan mountain? In search for wisdom!

The sages of the Himalayas, how come they go up into the Himalayas? In search for wisdom! So we know going up means knowledge; going up for the wisdom; to get the wisdom, to get the insight, the keys, the logic. Moses went up into the mountain and he came back with the laws written on the tablet. And those laws represent logic. They were the logic for a new order. And Moses is called the teacher. So when Jesus goes up, when he's crucified and he's put up, then he dies. So what is this symbolic of? This is symbolic of the history of Jesus' followers. Not Jesus. They didn't crucify Jesus. The history of Jesus' followers, when Jesus was gone, then what did they do? They tried to find Jesus. They tried to establish Jesus. They tried to establish what Jesus taught and for trying to do that, they were persecuted in the world and the world rejected them. They were not allowed to practice that in the government in the society. So that means being killed in the world. In the ninth hour they died and they went up. Say, "They put him up on a cross." Putting him up on a cross, what do you mean putting him up on a cross? The cross, then, represents, I said, the behavioral nature. So they tried to crucify him, bind him to his behavioral nature.

Now listen, please listen! They tried to bind him to his behavioral nature. Why would you bind something to his behavioral nature? Why do you want to do that? So that you'll never gain intellectual insight; so his behavioral nature is excellent. Let's make him the subject of his

Imam W. Deen Mohammed

behavioral nature. Let's make him so attached to his behavioral nature that he wants no more than that. He just wants to be good. Let me tell you something. You have to stretch your imagination to see the depths of Satan. Our little minds can't see it. We can't even think to do things this devilish; we can't even think, our imagination won't even stretch. It takes a scientific mind that's wicked to stretch to do such devilishment. So here is a man, a sign of the people. Now G-d sent a man into the world to liberate people to bring them into moral freedom and the process, that process is to bring them to the door of intellectual insight so that they will really gain that dignity on earth and here, the world plots against them. The wicked world plots against them and tries to contain them, bind them, with the rope of their own excellence.

The Quran and
Prophet Mohammed ﷺ

Prophet Mohammed ﷺ, during the wars with the oppressors, the persecutors of the religion, Islam - the Prophet ﷺ instructed his soldiers concerning trees, vegetation, not to destroy the crops, the food that the people have to live on and he instructed them not to do damage to trees. Here we see a commander of a society, a state and an army of that state instructing his soldiers to be respectful of vegetation and the needs of the people, though they were enemy people who had to subsist or who had to survive upon those resources, those plants or vegetation. He also instructed them not to destroy trees. The trees that he mentioned were not fruit bearing trees. They were trees, just trees of beauty. So here in this modern day and time, we find that man has now taken up these concerns as real issues; has brought them before government, before heads of state. They have discussed these issues and made it now law that you are not to kill or destroy certain life that is seen as useful to the environment of man or helpful for the environment of man. That's something that is appreciated by human beings, by humanity; beauty as a means of life, for livelihood. The government now has taken steps, as we know, for some years against the free destruction of these things of life and beauty. Muslims should take a special pride in knowing, that fourteen hundred years ago, when most of the world was in what we call the dark ages, at a time when modern man says this earth was under darkness and ignorance and given to savage and warring people, oppressors; Mohammed the Prophet ﷺ, the true liberator was preaching these modern concepts of respect for life, respect for things of beauty and respect for the needs of the people. Praise be to Allah. This religion is much more advanced, far advanced over all the knowledge and the civilizations that we know. In fact, it is the true leader. Nations don't always give this religion credit, but actually, the Qur'an and Prophet Mohammed ﷺ is the true leader that has led civilization and progress for humanity. Whatever else has made contributions, their contribution have been, I would say, additional help and the Qur'an and the life of Prophet Mohammed ﷺ had to even make those contributions acceptable or presentable (that they get from old scriptures other than Qur'an).

Scriptures that came before; Christian scriptures, Judeo Christian scriptures and from the Greek philosophers, without the help of Al-Islam, the Qur'an, Prophet

Mohammed ﷺ, they wouldn't have even been able to

appreciate what they found in old Greek knowledge or old

Greek science and what they had in the Bible, because the

Bible was present with them for those centuries before

Prophet Mohammed ﷺ and still they fell under what we

called the dark ages. So, praise be to Allah for blessing us

with the messenger Mohammed ﷺ, to whom this

Qur'an was revealed, and establishing him as a model

person for all people who would follow him. Prophet

Mohammed ﷺ, in his private life, he was seen as a

compassionate person, tender hearted person, loving

person, caring for big matters and small matters and never

giving himself to any extremism. He was not a man who

gave himself to any kind of extremism. He wouldn't even

laugh in extremes. He wouldn't weep in the extreme. He

did nothing in the extreme. He did not allow his passions

to take him into any extremes and this is what Muslims

have to know and have to practice. We are not to allow our

passions to take us to any extreme. Now that goes for any

situation. In war, Muslims are not to allow their passions

to take them to extremes. We know, when you get in war,

the pressure and force of passions can take your senses away and fighters forget their senses and they begin to slaughter as mad animals. Civilized war conduct does not allow such and Prophet Mohammed صلى الله عليه وسلم did not allow such on the part of Muslims. In fact, the rule was that there should be no maiming of any individual. Many charges have been made against the Muslim community, against Prophet Mohammed صلى الله عليه وسلم and the Muslim community, against this religion and we know them to be false. For what is established in the Qur'an, in the life of the Prophet صلى الله عليه وسلم, we are not to give ourselves to such extremes.

Prophet Mohammed صلى الله عليه وسلم says, "do not maim," and the Qur'an says, "do not mutilate" and even the westerners, they themselves, recognized this principle that's upheld in Al-Islam by the early Muslims under our Prophet when they put out the movie, Saladin. Saladin, the movie showed a Muslim warrior; this was long after Prophet Mohammed صلى الله عليه وسلم, centuries after Prophet Mohammed صلى الله عليه وسلم – showed a Muslim warrior fighting non-Muslims, fighting Europeans. The Europeans, their weapons were weapons of cruelty. In that movie you'll see the weapons that were popular in those days; they had balls and chains, they had a huge sword with a very wide blade, they had hatchets, they had cruel instruments of war. But, if you saw the movie, the warring Muslims, they had very sharp swords and thin civilized swords. Saladin's sword was very light and very thin and in the movie (I don't know if their sword was this sharp), but in the movie they showed the sharpness of Saladin's sword. I think it was Richard the Lionheart, he showed the power of his big heavy sword; big thing standing about this high – big cross looking thing, about six inches wide in the blade and he showed the power of his, he took it and broke a bar with it. Then Saladin he showed the power of his. He threw up a silk handkerchief and just held his blade out and the handkerchief split into two pieces when it fell down upon the blade. Now that was western presentation of the Muslim way. And we know from the principles of Al-Islam that even if you slaughter animals, Prophet Mohammed ﷺ said, "When you slaughter animals, use a very sharp knife so that you will not cause undue suffering to that animal." Use a very sharp knife; so we are not people given to cruelty and we protect our passions against such. Praise be to Allah!

There was a practice in the days of jahiliyyah, that age of darkness, in Arabic it's called jahiliyyah (it means the age of ignorance) that involved marksmanship, and the animals were the victims. They would tie an animal up and then the archer would practice shooting the animal. Prophet Mohammed ﷺ stopped them from doing such because that was a sport; cruel to the animal. This gives us some knowledge of Prophet Mohammed ﷺ. Now how, in the light of these facts, of Prophet Mohammed ﷺ, can we accept his enemies picture of him that show him as a warring maniac, a fanatic, a spiritual dreamer who was given to fanaticism and who persecuted the Christians and the Jews because they wouldn't accept his faith and who slaughtered them if they wouldn't profess the faith or made them become converts at the point of the sword. Westerners have written these things and we know them to be all lies; lies against the greatest model of human excellence ever to live on this planet earth and the one for all of us to copy now and in the future. Praise be to Allah

Imam W. Deen Mohammed

Dear beloved Muslims, we should be aware that every chapter of the Qur'an, opens with the words, "with Allah's name, the gracious, the compassionate, ar-Rahman ar-Rahim. Bismillah, ar-Rahman, ar-Rahim – that's how it opens, with the two great attributes of divine being, of divine creator, G-d, ar-rahman ar-rahim. In my study of the term ar-rahman, I have come upon some evidence that ar-rahman is the name that was used for G-d before the Qur'an was revealed. We know that Allah was also known to the Arabs before the Qur'an was revealed, however this name Allah was taken as a G-d that was all inclusive and they had made themselves private gods to whom they gave daily devotion but Allah was far away from them because he was not a private G-d. With the coming of the revelation to Prophet Mohammed ﷺ it was revealed that the only G-d is this G-d that is all inclusive and is far away from you and that you should remove all the private deities that you have fashioned with your own minds and with your own hands. Thereafter Allah became the only G-d of that vicinity we call Arabia and now that concept has spread all over the world almost with a membership of better than one billion people. Praise be to Allah.

What we are to understand here is that this religion invites us to the best conduct. It invites us to the best sentiments of man. Every chapter opens Bismillah – who is G-d? Ar-rahman, who is ar-rahman? It is answered in the Qur'an, "he who taught the Qur'an. He created the human being and taught him the balanced road." Praise be to Allah and then it goes on to tell us more about ar-rahman. "He's the one who put rich minerals and the pearls, etc. into the sea and has given you riches of two kinds. So, it goes on to tell us about ar-rahman. So, from the Qur'an we reason without necessarily giving back to the meanings that was before Qur'an when ar-rahman was in existence in that part of the land. We can go directly to the Qur'an now and we see from this way that Qur'an explains ar-rahman; ar-rahman is the merciful and generous G-d, because what is said of ar-rahman in the chapter, ar-rahman tells us that his quality stands out as mercy and generosity; that he has given us much more than we even can consume, given us much more than we even can use and he has shown mercy on us. He has come to our rescue when nothing else was able to help us. So we know that ar-rahman means the generous and merciful G-d. And ar-rahim means the one who continues that. He brings it about again. He renews it. That is repeated over and over again. If he comes to man's aid and man loses the way, he returns to man again, -in time. He has shown this mercy and grace through man, as a conscious being and through man as just another created product.

Many Imams have pointed to the recognition of this attribute of G-d in the creation of the female. The female who is born like the male and she comes into her maturity and becomes a wife and becomes pregnant with child and before the child is born, G-d has already caused that female to love that child. The child is not born. She's never seen the child but already she's fallen in love with that child. And G-d, before the child is delivered, forms food near so the mother won't have to go looking for food. He brings food out of her body; not late, in time!

So the learned in this religion, among the scholars and Imams, they have pointed to this as a sign of ar-rahim, ar-rahim. G-d is ar-rahman, and being that way to man through his intellect, through his conscious, but he is rahim in doing that through the processes of nature and these processes of nature are repeated and we should understand – just as the processes of nature are repeated, the social

process is repeated, too. Therefore, Allah is ar-rahim as
well as ar-rahman. And every time we open a chapter, we
have to say Bismillah, ar-rahman ar-rahim. We're
reminded before reading any chapter that our G-d is
merciful and generous and that he repeats and continues
that generosity. He has it as an eternal process though the
sinners disrespect G-d's gifts and man falls under the
oppression of the sinners and becomes a savage, lost in his
way, G-d will bring that back to him just as a little baby.
Reduce him to a little baby and then when he looks for the
food, there it will be just like the milk in the mother's
breast and there will be compassion for him in a cruel
environment. G-d will bring compassion to him again.

This is Allah, and the Prophet ﷺ has taught us, that we
are to imbue, we are to take on, to dye ourselves, to
saturate ourselves, to color ourselves with the attributes of
G-d. And he has taught with his mouth that as Allah is ar-
rahman, we are to be also. Rahman – merciful! Although
we are not G-d, but we are to be merciful since G-d is ar-
rahman. As G-d is ar-rahman ar-rahim, we are to be
merciful. And G-d is generous, we are to be generous. As
G-d is knowing, we are to be knowledgeable. The Prophet
ﷺ has taught us this; how we should relate to the

attributes of G-d. And whereas these things in G-d are divine and perfect, in man, they are a learning process and they are growth that continues and brings them to better and better life and better and better states of development. Praise be to Allah.

Only one chapter does not open with Bismillah ar-rahman ar-rahim and within the context of that chapter these attributes are given. So though it doesn't open with it, they are in the chapter; meaning that this is one time in man's life when G-d does not respond to him but eventually he comes around without G-d; ar-rahman ar-rahim – he comes around. Hell brings him around! It's not by the mercy of G-d, but hell brings him around and then after he comes around, then he will see ar-rahman ar-rahim. So that's why it's inside the contents of that chapter. Praise be to Allah. And you know that chapter is numbered, chapter nine, tawbah, and tawbah means repentance. That means that's the time when G-d won't come to you until you repent, because you're clearly in the wrong. It's different when we're the victim of wrongdoing, but when we, ourselves, are the wrongdoer, then G-d doesn't come to us with merciful tenderness. He lets hell teach us a lesson and we'll come around. Allah says, "Hellfire brings around men and stones." He says of the flame, "that he engulfs them in flames or entombs them in flames that break up." In other words, if you think you're so stubborn and tight together, then wait for those flames. They will break you up and I've seen great fires break up stones. I've been told to stand back, the stones are popping and you might be hit by a flying stone – great fire was burning up the matter and breaking up stones. We know, also, that G-d has said, "Nine wicked men were in the city." So this nine is associated with wicked people; so we shouldn't expect the nine wicked men in the city to say Bismillah ar-rahman ar-rahim until hell gets the better of them.

It has been said, and they continue to say it, the Qur'an teaches the Muslim that his religion is to dominate all other peoples' religion and that they are to conduct jihad or war on people until everybody confess or profess Muslim religion. The very source or verse that they quote from says, "And fight them, slay them, until there be no more persecution and religion be free for G-d." Nowhere in what they quote is anything given for them to base that kind of claim on. It doesn't say, slay the Christians and the Jews, or slay any religious people by name. And it says, "And slay them until there is no more persecution." And the word that is used for persecution, the Arabic word is fitna! And Allah says of this particular fitna, "and surely the fitna is a greater, and surely this fitna is a worse crime against people than outright slaughtering them." So here, Al-Islam uses fighting, slaughtering in war, killing in war to stop a bigger injustice. In fact, killing when you're stopping a wrong is not an injustice; it's a mercy. If a wild group of people would attack us right now, break in these doors and attack us and we would kill them, would that be killing or saving life. That would be saving life. If you have cruel persecutors who torture people because they believe in Allah, who deprive people of their freedom because they believe in Allah, who rob them of their possessions, boycott them and give them a miserable life because they believe in G-d and if you rise up with an army and fight those people until they stop doing that, are you killers or liberators? The truth stands by itself. So G-d says, "Fight them and slay them wherever you find them until the war lays down its burden." What is the burden? Justice! Until justice is had! When justice is had, ok, you can stop fighting. So many verses in this Qur'an – why do they go to one verse, one little place in Qur'an to say that

Al-Islam or Mohammed ﷺ, or the Qur'an advocate this kind of cruel oppression of people who believe in a religion other than ours. Why do they go to one little verse and then misinterpret and mis-present it? Present it out of context, pass over the many, many, many verses that they must have read, looking for that that says, "Let there be no compulsion in religion. Let no one be forced in religion." That says, "Whoever has a will to believe, let him believe and whoever has a will to disbelieve let him disbelieve." Say, "Surely right is established and is seen plainly from wrong. So let him who wants to, take a way that is straight." This is the teaching of Qur'an from cover to cover. Say to the disbelievers, "I do not believe in what you believe in, and you're not inclined to believe in what I believe in. And I'm not inclined to believe in what you believe in. For you is your way or your religion and for me is my religion." What is that saying? Say, "go about your business if you don't believe in Al-Islam. Nobody is forcing anybody to be Muslims. Never did and never will! We're Muslims in America. Here's the proof for Americans. We're Muslims in America. Nobody forced Imam Warith Deen Mohammed to become a Muslim and Imam Mohammed, he never forced anybody to accept this

65

religion. He does not even call for a show of hands, say, who's ready to confess today? No! That's your business. You know when you're ready! So nobody would keep this evil idea of our Prophet and our religion in the hearts except one who's a devil or diseased by the devil.

Let's go now to chapter surah Luqman, chapter Luqman; the second section of the chapter beginning with the twelfth verse. Allah, most high, says, "We certainly have bestowed on Luqman wisdom, saying, show gratitude to G-d. And who is so grateful does so to the profit to his own soul. But if any is ungrateful, verily G-d is free of all wants and worthy of all praise." What does that say? Does that say, if anyone does not wish to thank G-d, do not wish to recognize G-d, that he's going to be forced to? No! It says whoever appreciates G-d, appreciates G-d to the benefit or to the profit of himself and whoever shows ungratefulness, should know that G-d doesn't need him. That's what this says; that surely G-d is free of all wants. You're not giving him anything by being appreciative. He's not going to be made richer or made better or stronger, or more G-d because you like him. See, we can't talk independent like this; we're his creatures, but we who

represent him and like to get on your case for being
ungrateful and ignorant, we get a great satisfaction by
telling you G-d doesn't need anything from you! If you
like him it's to your own benefit. If you dislike him you
take nothing from him. And I think he didn't have to tell
us that. I think he told us that so we won't be affected
when people don't want G-d or when they don't want
Allah and they don't want the Qur'an, they don't want
Prophet Mohammed ﷺ. He's telling us that so we won't
be affected. You don't want him; see you later! Goodbye!
Sorry I saw you this time! So long you unpleasant sight! I
don't know why the sinners like to be begged, but most of
the sinners – they want to be begged. "I'll stop sinning if
you beg me long enough!" "I might change my faith, and
become this, if you beg me long enough!" You're the one
that needs to repent. You should be the one begging.

The next verse of this chapter says (that is Luqman to his
son by way of divine instruction), "oh, my son, join not in
worship others with the G-d (with Allah with the one G-d)
for false worship is indeed the highest wrong doing." Now
we're going to continue this advice of Luqman for the
whole section here, chapter 12 to chapter 13 and we're

going to come back to verse thirteen where it says, "surely, shirk, associating others with the one G-d as G-d, is the greatest of all wrong doing." And we have enjoined on man;" this is the fourteenth verse, "and we have enjoined on man to do good, to be good to his parents. In travail upon travail did his mother bare him," travail means pain, stress, agony and weak spells because of the severity of the hardship, even fainting; and in two years was his weaning." Hear the command? Show gratitude to me and to your parents; to me is your final goal." This is what G-d says in the Qur'an. Now look! The G-d that says, "Be grateful to G-d." Then comes back behind saying, "be grateful to G-d" and says, "Be grateful to me and your parents." So this is not a G-d that just wants converts. He wants children to love and respect the parents that he has made for their care and for their livelihood, for their subsistence, etc., in their weak state, until they're adults or able to manage for themselves. This G-d wants to care for his life that he created. He does not want just conversion.

I have read from the western people's scriptures that they read, where it says that he comes for the purpose of breaking up families. You will find nothing like that anywhere in this religion; talking about G-d came for the purpose of breaking up families – setting father against son, the mother against daughter, etc. That's the language of their scripture. Now, suppose the Muslims were dirty like they are and would dig up all that dirt and would publicize it and turn people against them like they try to turn people against the Muslims. Why, after a while there would be a court to outlaw that religion. If we were to really wage a strong campaign against it, there would be a universal court of man and outlaw the religion. But G-d has given them mercy. Say, come on, one day they will see. The Prophet ﷺ was told, "Go easy on them, spare them, be easy with them." In another place, Allah says in the Qur'an, "and there will come a time, there will come a day when they will be shown."

In the Bible it says, "Those who live in glass houses should not throw stones." And they don't even read it themselves. You're in a glass house and you threw a stone at somebody else. If they throw stones back, your glass will come down on you. You get cut up by your own glass. And the next verse, the fifteenth verse, it says, "but if they strive to make you join in worship with me things of which

69

you have no knowledge, obey them not." Here is the balanced religion. G-d told Prophet Mohammed ﷺ to be merciful and kind to his creatures and to respect everything. This is the teachings of Qur'an to Prophet Mohammed ﷺ and to us and told him to be soft and gentle, and says, that when you protest, protest in a manner that is good, most excellent. Even when you protest! "And when you protest before them, do it in a way that is good and most excellent." This is Qur'an; but the same Qur'an, the same Allah that tells the Prophet ﷺ and tells us to be easy and take care and be tender and caring, even when we're dealing with our enemies it also says, "And fight them and pursue them in the fight until the war lays down its burden." This is when you're dealing with merciless people; savage, cruel, oppressive people; don't be tender with them. You let them know you can deal with them. And then another situation says when the Muslim breaks the law of Al-Islam, being guilty of major sin, adultery, fornication and the like, punish them. Discipline them before the witnesses, and don't let the tenderness of your heart cause you to be light in the punishment because that's a situation when you have to be firm. You can discipline him and the man might cry out and touch your heart. You might start crying with him, and most of the wrong people, they're better at deceiving us with their emotions than the good people. Good people don't have deceitful emotions. People who know they're wrong and know they're going to continue to be wrong, they practice deceiving you with their emotions. So you discipline the person, and you know they might make you feel like you're cruel, but discipline him and you'll see the real emotions come out. His emotions will be purified. What is this message saying? This message is saying that you have to be intelligent in this religion and you have to obey G-d. You can't allow your emotions to take you away from what is just and what is right because, if you do that makes you putty-brained, silly-minded and you will never be strong enough to manage society. You'll always have to be the ward of somebody else in the society. But if you can see intelligently what is proper and most excellent for human life and carry that out even when your own heart is hurt by it.

You think a mother enjoys disciplining her children? No, a normal mother does not enjoy disciplining her children, but she disciplines them. If she would let her heart tell her what to do, she wouldn't discipline her child. Oh, well maybe I'm a little wrong there. The heart does tell her what to do; but the heart it speaks to two situations. The heart speaks to the hurt and the heart speaks to the justice and the mother, she has to be a wise enough judge to ignore what the heart is saying about the hurt until she carries out justice. Now if she carries justice beyond justice, where the punishment becomes cruelty, then she has to listen to the heart speaking to her on the hurt. Now, that's an illustration, but the pure guidance is in the Qur'an.

I just gave you an example from human experience that says very clearly to any of our silly minds, (no matter how stupid we are) that administering punishment requires firmness; firmness on the part of the administrator of that punishment. You have to be firm. Don't obey yourself, obey justice! Don't obey yourself, obey Allah! Don't obey yourself, obey Mohammed ﷺ! Obey the Sunnah of the Prophet ﷺ, because if you obey yourself, you're too weak. You're too weak to administer justice. You're going to get into a situation where you care too much about the

person that should be punished and if you obey yourself,
you're going to do an injustice and you'll come into a
situation where you are prejudiced against the person and
have hateful feelings toward that person and you'll then go
beyond the limits of the law and you will punish that
person too much. So you have to not obey self. Obey the
law of justice and obey the spirit of the law, for with every
order of punishment, that administers punishment in this
Qur'an G-d seasons it with a reminder of his mercy, his
justice of good sense, etc.

So what are we saying? Most of us can't administer
justice! Most of us cannot administer justice even in our
homes. We wrong our children either by spoiling them and
letting them go too far or by being too hard, too cruel.
What is the answer? Learn the rules and regulations given
to us in the Qur'an and learn the spirit of the Qur'an, the
spirit of the law and the Qur'an and learn the life of
Prophet Mohammed ﷺ and how he administered the
justice of the Qur'an. Then you'll become a good father, a
good mother, a good big brother, a good sister, a good
aunt, etc. But until then, if you're trusting only yourself,
you're in danger. If you aren't careful, you're going to

Imam W. Deen Mohammed

send children to jail, send them to crime, to death, or either they're going to lock you up for abusing your children. You can't do it by yourself. That's why we have such a problem in this society. Crime, permissiveness, child abuse, wife abuse, husband abuse, homosexual abuse, every abuse!

Yes, we continue now. Say's, "if the parents strive with you to make you worship with G-d other than something that is not G-d, says, obey them not and the verse goes on, "yet bear them company in this life with justice and consideration and keep company with them in the world. We witness that G-d is G-d. There is nothing like unto him. There is no partner with him in the rule or in the run of the heavens and the earth, and we witness that Mohammed is his servant and his messenger, the prayers and the peace be upon him and what follows of the traditional salutation or salute to Mohammed ﷺ, the last Prophet.

23rd Seerah Conference
12-25-2005

بسم الله الرحمن الرحيم

Imam W. Deen Mohammed

Today is Christmas; 25th of December. It's always on the
25th. They taught me my tables when I was in school, five
times five is twenty five; that five runs its course. When
you say five times six you're out of five, you're
somewhere else. Christ Jesus, he saw a woman at the well
and said, "woman you've had five husbands over you and
the one you've got now, is not yours." Merry Christmas
everybody and a Happy New Year! If you can make it
through Christmas you'll have a Happy New Year, won't
you? Tomorrow, everybody is broke. Now that's Wallace
talking. My Imam is getting ready to speak.

Mohammed the Prophet ﷺ is our topic, our subject for
the rest of these minutes, or hours that I have here and we
want to begin by saying that G-d himself identifies his last
Prophet, the final Prophet, the seal of the Prophets; he
identifies him and before we say anything about him, we
must go to what G-d says about him and G-d says, "We
have not sent you to be any other than a mercy to all the
worlds" and it goes on. And of the Prophet ﷺ it is said
in the Qur'an, that the Prophet ﷺ is a free person in the

76

city. Now, at that time, he was being persecuted by his own people and they were in the stronger position in terms of might, physical power, etc. Men, fighters and all that, and he was guided by G-d to say to the people, "I am a free man in this city or a free person in this city." And then we have also in the Qur'an, much later in his mission, he is told to "fight that opposition; to fight them. Fight them until there is no more persecution." So why was he fighting them? He was fighting them because they were persecuted. It's clear that he was only fighting because he and his followers were persecuted. "Fight them until there is no more persecution and the war put down its arms." And again, and it says, "and religion in free for G-d." That means religion is serving G-d, religion is there to serve G-d; there for G-d, not for the king.

Do you know many countries, in fact the world; the past, that's behind us; religion served the king. Religion served the ruler, whoever the ruler was; religion was serving him to keep the people in order. To keep the people not rebelling. Religion was serving the king, and in the world right now, religion, in many places is protecting whoever that ruler is. King, or president or whatever he is. Religion is protecting him by keeping the masses peaceful or keeping them focused on G-d and on obeying G-d. So religion was used to keep the publics of these kings, these rulers, in check; so that they wouldn't bother the king or the ruler. So this is how religion was used in the past. These old nations, these old empires, old governments, they were persecutors of the human spirit. When I say persecutors of the human spirit, I hope all of you understand. If I was speaking to the students of theology, etc., they would, I wouldn't have to explain a thing to them when I say persecutors of the human spirit, they know exactly what I am saying. In case some of you don't know what I'm saying, I'll explain to you. Allah created every human being to want to be right. We go wrong. We except to do wrong, some of us, but Allah created every human person with a will, or spirit, to do what is right, and Allah created every human with a will or spirit to want to see right done by others, not just by themselves, but also done by others; who want to see justice, fairness, want to see kindness and mercy given to those who deserve it. This is the soul that Allah made – the creator. That's every baby; it comes in here with a soul like that, and loses it to the bad influences in the world, or in their surroundings. In other words, for Muslim language, as the Prophet ﷺ said,

"Every human person is born Muslim and it is the circumstances that they're in that makes them different." This is His words to the Prophet ﷺ. So these rulers, if they're to survive, they have to have something to hold the people against their very nature that G-d created them with. They have to have something to hold the people. So religion has served that purpose. We know these rulers are oppressors and they oppress, and they are terrible. They hold down the good life and keep the good life from the many and give it only to those that serve their interests. We know that, but they're oppressors, we have to say, they're terrible oppressors, tyrants, bad people with power. But Allah doesn't say Pharaoh is the worst oppressor. Allah says, "Surely, false worship is the worse form of oppression." So, we find in the Qur'an G-d describing Mohammed the Prophet ﷺ, and he describes him

saying, "He is the unlettered Prophet." He is the unlettered Prophet in the Torah and in the Injil. That is in the books, that came to Moses and in the Gospel that is claimed for Jesus Christ – the Gospel, the New Testament; that he is in both books. Now, how is he in both books? I found him in the old books. I found the reference, because Allah tells us what he will do in the Qur'an. It says what he will do. Say,

"He will take the heavy yokes off their back." Off the back; that means you can't see it. Something on your back you aren't looking at it. He would take the heavy yoke off their back.

You're getting special things here. There are wise people in the top of religion, life of the world, that would be very much thrilled to hear me say what I just said and they would be rushing up to me when I conclude, to tell me how much they have been helped by what I just said. But you all don't know, so it's just like a visitor from Mars or something coming here and you don't know. Allah identifies him, he says, "he is the one in the Torah and in the Injil; the one who would take the heavy burden from the backs – the heavy yoke that weights the back down and breaks every bond of slavery." Free all slaves; break every bond of slavery. He's the one. Now, this is the liberator, isn't it? So Allah gives Prophet Mohammed ﷺ to us as a liberator. He's a liberator and since this is a religion, he's a liberator also for religion. He's freeing religion; not only freeing people, but he's freeing religion. I hope you understand and it's clear! If you don't strain your mind too much, it's clear. So this is the Prophet ﷺ mentioned, but

80

how is he in the New Testament? I'll just come right out and tell you! That's why I said Merry Christmas. Jesus Christ, the same figure is in the New Testament and he's the subject of the New Testament from beginning to end – Jesus Christ came in the world as a sign of the coming of the truth from G-d and that truth will conquer all falsehood. He was a sign of that - truth is coming into the world from G-d and it's going to conquer all falsehood. Allahu-Akbar!

See when I go as far as I can on a run, I have to get on another one. I'm on another run, now! G-d says to us in Qur'an, "that he is the one who provides for us from the earth and from the sky. He gives us our sustenance (I'm using that language of the translator now) both from the earth and from the sky. Now, from the earth, what is that? To save a lot of time I'm not going to give a lot of quotes and all that today, I'm going straight to the purpose; dealing straight with the purpose. So what does it mean when it says, G-d says that he gives us from the earth? What is the earth? Appetites! So G-d gives us what we need for our earthly appetites. Whatever we need for our earthly appetites – food, clothing, shelter, comforts of this reality, etc. But he also gives us from the sky. And what comes from the sky? We know rain! Well, rain is symbolic of revelation sometimes. So he gives us from the sky also rain, but rain comes from the lower sky, very low, really. The lowest of the sky is rain and we know other things; sometimes the sky will rain down material objects and sometimes we find after the objects have burned and cooled and are safe to go and pick up with our hands – precious metal comes down from the sky. So he also gives us material from the sky, too; not just water or spiritual. He also gives us material – sometimes from the sky. That's why he said, "G-d sends down iron!" It's in Qur'an. You who read the Qur'an, he sends down iron. Iron comes out of the sky. Now, we know that's a metaphor, or that's symbolic language that has to be understood. We know that, but it is also true in common language. We know that there have been objects that fell from the sky; fell to the earth from the sky and they found that there was iron in those objects. It had been heated up by the fire, falling through atmosphere and cooled off and there was iron left there in the hole that the comet made when it fell down into the earth. So, we know this is literally true, too and let me tell you something! Whatever Allah says in the Qur'an is true to your mind; that's uneducated, and true to the

mind educated in the language of revelation – it has to be
true in both! So, if G-d says he's going to give you pure
virgins, he means that! The pure one's they will get pure
virgins; he means that! You probably can't handle seventy
two of them, but it says seventy two. Now, that's the part
you need to interpret, but not the virgins, you going to get
some virgins down here and it says the worthy. The virgin
man is worthy of the virgin woman and vice-versa. The
virgin woman is worthy of the virgin man, but we know on
this sensual level, or this sensuous level; that's the
cheapest reward. The more expensive reward is on the
level of the translation and interpretation. And the
hereafter is more valuable, more precious, more valuable
both in quantity and in quality. This is G-d's word in the
Qur'an – both in quantity and in quality.

So, he's going to send from the sky? Will it be these
metals that fell from the sky? No! What is he going to give
us from the sky to govern our appetites? He's going to
fulfill our appetites from the earth; to govern our appetites,
to survive our appetites? Don't you know man has to
survive his own appetites? His appetites will kill him and
you know that; many of you. Yes, the appetites will kill

him, and the appetites will get him killed. Both! Appetites will kill him and appetites will get him killed because, if he wants what I've got I might kill him. But if he just wants without bothering me, he might kill himself; consuming too much, or consuming the wrong thing. So it's not talking about that. The earth gets to fulfill that, our appetites. So what is he going to give us from the sky? Perception!

You students, please write that down. Perception! The clear perception that will free the life down on earth, is the perception we get from the sky. In the Arabic poem, he's saying, "the night has a thousand eyes and the day, but one" - talking about the sun and the thousand, talking about the stars. Well, actually we know it's more than a thousand, but he said that just to make a picture, give a picture comparison; said the night has a thousand eyes and the day but one. The poet says the night has eyes means that the night has light and when you understand those lights, it will open your eyes to a bigger reality. So it is the heavens that opens our eyes to the bigger reality. We will never know this system of matter unless we study the sky. And you can't see the sky until the sun has gone. The sun sets and darkness prevails, and then we can see on a clear night, when there's no clouds in the lower heavens – we can see a big space up there that, right away, tells us that space is much bigger than our space down here. Right away, common persons know that. Right away the space up there is much bigger than the space down here – and so many lights – filled with lights. And the farther you look and the deeper you go you still see signs of more lights behind those lights. And they invent the telescope and they revealed the lights that we couldn't see with our eyes, many lights out there, that we couldn't ever reach with our eyes. They invent the telescope and make it powerful enough to see beyond what we can see and even the telescope reaches its end, and the telescope, just like the eye, sees there's more lights behind the lights that it can't see too well. So we know that we cannot reach the end of the lights. We can't reach the end of space. Man has progressed to this degree that he has progressed in science, technology, but he cannot give anybody on earth a map of the universe because he's steadily seeing, tuning his glass to see farther and farther away and every time he gets a high powered glass to see further away, he's see more stars. He doesn't know the end of it, so he can't give us a map of this reality. He can't give us a map of the creation itself and some of you all want to see the ends of G-d. You want to see where G-d starts and stops. First see where his world starts and stop that you're living on, that you're living in – see where it starts and stops. You can't see that and none of your highest scientists can see that. The United States can't see that and you know that's a bad boy isn't it? It can't give us a map of the universe. It only can give us a map of what is known to them so far – what's known to science so far. That's all they can give us. That's a reality that ought to humble you and stop you from asking disrespectful questions of G-d – disrespecting your G-d; asking stupid questions.

So from the heavens comes perception. How are we to pinpoint this so we know, in fact, what this is all about, the Prophet Abraham is our second father, and he's called second father because he earned it from G-d. G-d saw him in his constitution, in his mental makeup, and his mind, his thoughts, and in his interests, his heart, what his heart was interested in and G-d loved him in that form and even called him a friend. And G-d gave him the title, "Imam for all nations. Imam for all people" and according to the Prophet Mohammed ﷺ, G-d also established him as our second father, Abraham. Mohammed ﷺ established that

when he reported to his following, and to the world, what

he experienced on his ascent from the Ka'bah up into the

heavens; his travels, the night travel from the vicinity of

Mecca, or the Ka'bah, to the distant mosque. Al-Aqsa-the

distant mosque. So he reported what he saw and when he

was taken up he saw Adam on the first level. Ascending up

into the heavens, he saw Adam, our first father, on the first

level and he greets him to let us know how we are to

recognize Adam. He said, "Peace be on you, my father

Adam and every other level he ascended, he met Prophets

and he would greet them the same, (but he wouldn't say

father, he said brother). My brother this, my brother that

until he reached the 7th heaven and he met Abraham there

and he greeted him, too (father). He said, "Peace be on you

my father Abraham." You won't find this in the Qur'an.

This is given so that we'll know that we are, as followers

of Prophet Mohammed ﷺ, we are to recognize Jesus

Christ and we'll recognize Adam, and we are to recognize

all the others, and we are to recognize the last, the 7th

heaven, Abraham, is the highest heaven – Abraham! We

are to recognize them and know that two of those are our

fathers; the father of mankind, Adam – the first one – the

mortal, Adam and the last one, the intellect, Ibrahim. Yes! Allahu-Akbar!

So, how did the sky serve Abraham? Abraham was trying to find truth; truth to free his heart and his soul and put his mind in a situation to grow as it would please him. The thinkers, we call them free thinkers, in the history of the development of the world. The free thinker, he is pondering, or thinking on what he's observing in the real world – everything in his environment, including himself. He's thinking, "how did this come about, and what is the purpose of this? He wants to understand, he wants an understanding for his mind and his soul. So he's thinking on these things. So Abraham, he left his own father (now don't say he left his father, too - no, that has got nothing to do with little Wallace. We've got something bigger than little Wallace right now.) So he left his own father because his own father was worshiping things that the little young Abraham couldn't accept; and he couldn't accept it because he followed common sense. Common sense told him that those things that his people made should not be authorities in his life and he shouldn't trust those things that his people made with their hands and called gods; he

shouldn't trust them with his hopes, his wishes and his life.
So he actually destroyed the idols; broke them up – and his
father heard that his son did that, so he came to his son and
said, "Did you do this, Abraham?" And he said, "Ask the
biggest one who did it!" So his father was very much
insulted and rational quickly ran its course and he told his
son, "get out; you're abandoned from this kingdom – you
cannot stay in this kingdom!" So he drove him out of the
kingdom that he was in. He had to go to other countries
and really, I think that was the way G-d freed him. G-d –
that was his first step to freeing him. G-d wanted to put
him out into his own land and make him go where
strangers live.

So he went to strange lands and everywhere he went he
was honorable and upright. This is the Bible. Everywhere
he went he was truthful, honorable and upright. So, one
day, according to the Qur'an, he was searching the
universe to the outer boundaries of the creation, to see if he
could find, "what should I recognize as G-d", and you
know how the story goes (some of you). When night fell,
he saw the stars and they were all beautiful and appealing
to him but once he saw a star fall, he said, "no, stars cannot

be my G-d, for my G-d does not fall." Now, he hadn't
even met with G-d yet, but the human being is given
common sense, common human sense told him, "I
shouldn't worship something that's dying and falling out
of the sky, light going out." He wants something that'll
stay lit eternally, that'll serve him eternally. He's not just
looking for something for Abraham's light, he's looking
for something that'll serve mankind forever on this planet
earth. That's what he was looking for. So he rejected the
stars as being G-d and he stayed until the night passed and
the sun started to rise. And its light, from our situation as
human beings, the sunlight seemed so much nearer and so
it seemed so much bigger than the objects out there afar,
because their being so far away, they appeared to be
smaller than our sun. Science has revealed to us, we know
that there are objects out there much bigger than our sun –
much, much bigger that our sun, but we can't tell that. We
can't know that with the ordinary vision on the human eye.
You have to have a telescope and scientific thinking to
discover that. So, anyway, the sun came up big and he
said, "oh, look how splendid this one is, rising in its glory.
How splendid it is. How bright and beautiful!" He
continued to watch it. It rose up to noon and it started to
decline; and it declined and it went out. Then he said, "I

witness that the one behind all of this is G-d; that none of
this world is G-d, but there is something behind it.
Something started all this and that is G-d!" So the Jews
and others, especially Jews and Muslims, we recognize
that Abraham is the one that came to the conclusion that
the creator, or the cause behind creation, the maker of all
this, is the only G-d – one G-d alone. So he gave us the
monotheistic idea in religion – Abraham. And when he
gave us that, he gave us much more than that (please
continue to listen and students please take notes, especially
when there is something that you know you need to hold.
Take notes).

He gave us, he gave the world, much more than just to
believe that there is one G-d. If Allah says (going back to
what I said earlier), "surely worshipping more than one
with G-d, (confusing the idea of G-d, putting something
with G-d), "surely this is a worst form of oppression."
What is it oppressing? Number one, it oppresses your
intelligence. It oppresses your good senses. It's going in
conflict with common, good sense that G-d gave you. So
it's going in conflict with the intelligence G-d created. G-d
created common sense. G-d created my common senses to

know that this is hot, this is cold. This is dangerous, this is
not. This is ugly. This is beautiful. This is hard. This is
soft. This is intelligent. This is not. G-d gave every human
being this sense. Now, when something goes against that
sense, you shouldn't accept it. I don't care what it is. If it's
Imam W. Deen Mohammed, if he goes against your good
common sense you shouldn't accept what he says, no. But
don't reject it just instantly, "oh, that's wrong." No,
because you could be wrong! But after you discuss it with
others who have good common sense and others that you
respect that are intelligent and you all come up with shurah
decision. Shurah, you have a shurah decision that this is
against good sense, good common sense, you should reject
it. I don't care where it comes from. You should reject it.

Now, continuing this line of discussion; when G-d says
that, "surely associating or confusing the idea of G-d is the
worst form of oppression," what is being oppressed?
Number one, your intelligence; your brain, your good
sense, number one is oppressed. If I can enslave your
brain, I can enslave everything else you've got; the way to
free the person is through the brain and the way to enslave
a person is through the brain. You can't enslave me until

you get my brain. You might lock me up and put shackles on me. I'm not a slave. The best part of me escapes shackles. The best part of me reaches out beyond prison walls and many men have been put in prison and come up with their best production while they were locked up. They wrote their best works. They left humanity that will advance humanity though they died in prison. Socrates was one of them. Yes, they arrested him and eventually killed him by poisoning him – gave him hemlock - what is hemlock? Blood lock! What is blood lock? Mind lock! So, what is the real death of Socrates? They prevented him from using his intelligence and passing his intelligence on to others. They locked it up so it couldn't get out to others. That was the real death.

That's the worst thing that they did to Socrates and that is how you should understand the crucifixion of Jesus Christ. They gave him acetic (this is the New Testament). Said, "And soon as he drank of the acetic, right away he gave up the spirit, the ghost, was dead." Acetic is a play on asceticism. So this is the way you have to understand these things and if you understand them this way, you'll be free. You'll be free indeed and you'll be in a good position to

Imam W. Deen Mohammed

have a good life and a pleasant life. Your life will be
relieved of a lot of burden, unnecessary burden, like that,
that weighs down the back; a load the animals carry. The
animal never sees the load; he just feels it on his back. You
know that some of the drug addicts say, "I'm carrying a
monkey on my back." So it was Abraham who really
liberated mankind; and Abraham there, is not a human
person; Abraham there, is a correct thinking for the free
thinker, personified in Abraham. Abraham is a
personification of the activities in the mind of the free
thinker that will take the world to where it has to go,
rationally speaking, intellectually speaking, spiritually
speaking. Praise be to Allah. So when you see the whole
universe then you say, "hey, this earth is small, this is just
a small thing in this big creation, or this big reality; earth is
a small thing." Then you become less home oriented. You
become less oriented as a member of a nation. Your
nationality becomes less important to you now than your
new perception of truth and reality. Not only your
nationality, but your tribe, your race all becomes less
important now than your new vision of truth and reality.
So you want to hurry up and share this with all people on
earth so they'll have a common agreement, where they
disagree, maybe in many things, but if all of us can see

94

what liberates all human minds and hearts, we can agree in one thing and that one thing is bigger than all of our small things, right? Because, this is the universe, not America, not the United States. This is not London; this is the universe we're talking about. It's much bigger than all of us. So, we can agree in what this bigger reality says to us. It speaks to us; it speaks to our intelligence; then we can all come together.

And this brings us to the next. This brings us to the connections that all agree in one pattern or one system. All of this world – the earth by itself, so small – like a speck that you can't find with your naked eye in the system of matter or the worlds. You can't find the earth unless you have a telescope and if you're far enough away, you can't even find the earth with the most powerful telescope that's in existence. This is the reality. So this little small world we live on, this small space we occupy here, we call earth, it has its systems. Not one, its systems; it has a system of material things, but it has also systems of energy. There are two realities – two main realities, material and then energy. And then it has another reality in it – design, because this matter has design. Now the design of one metal will be different from the design of another, but the design of matter is one. They have one common design, like we have one common human life. When you get hurt and you need blood, the doctor isn't going to say what's your race? No, you need blood. He isn't going to say I've got some Chinese blood here, what's your race? You need blood, you don't need Chinese blood, you need human blood. You don't need African blood, you need human blood. So the doctor isn't going to ask you what's your race, he's just going to give you some blood, and you're going to be alright. It's human blood. So we have one life in common, don't we? G-d has made us one life, one life in common. So we have one pattern in common, one design in common. When you go with a broken bone, the doctor isn't going to ask you, "What did you say you broke?" Oh, I broke my left arm - that's enough. The doctors going to go to that left arm. He isn't going to treat you like you're an octopus or something. He knows you aren't an octopus. You're a human being and he knows all human beings have a same left arm. A left arm is a left arm, so he'll go to the chart and will he say, "Give me an Egyptian chart of the human anatomy." No, the human anatomy chart is all the same; same for one man as it is for another. No matter what part of the world he's in. So this is universal, like this is one single life. What I'm getting at is this, just as we can find the true identity in one single pattern of life that makes us all the same species or the same creation, human creation, flesh creation, we can find, also, the unity of matter. The unity of matter that's true for all matter, whether it comes from up there in the skies or down here or anywhere, it's the same. What's that? The molecular construction, molecular structure of matter is the same for all matter. All matter is composed or consists of molecules; science of blood, science of everything in the human composition and then when you study the outer world, there's the science of geography, the science of geology, the science of astronomy; all these different sciences and the one who started all this process was Abraham.

Now, go back to the meaning I gave you of Abraham – not a person. Don't look for a Jew and don't look for an Arab. Look for the description I gave you of Abraham. So the prayer in Qur'an, Qur'anic Arabic; G-d is the one who impressed us with our paths. He says it in words and then he says, "And we would not have come to these paths, if you had not guided us." Here's what he said to G-d, "we would not have arrived at these paths, we would have not found these paths if you had not guided us."

What are these paths referring to? We have two roads in Islamic knowledge; two roads in Islamic religion. One is sirat al-mustaqeem. Now, what picture does that give us? The vertical picture – sirat al-mustaqeem – the vertical development or the vertical growth. Now a little comment on this: the vertical growth, going straight up like a tree – like the trunk of a tree, straight up and it's going straight up because it wants to keep its balance. It wants to carry the most weight. To carry the most weight, it has to grow straight up. If it leans, it won't be able to hold this much weight. The weight will, maybe, break it, bend it over or break it if it leans. It's got to go straight up so it can bear the most weight. Keep equilibrium, equal balance so it's going straight up. And you know, the loose street fellows (youngsters on the street), I remember a few years ago, they developed a new expression – "aw man, be straight up man." "Oh, I'm straight up, man!" You know! They developed that language and it means truthful, doesn't it? It means not deceiving – straight up! So, the mustaqeem is the road that goes straight up. When one asked for advice from the Prophet ﷺ, he said, "Give me something – tell

me something that no one but you can tell me." He

(Prophet) said, "Say I believe or I have believed and

thereafter be upright." And what was the Prophet ﷺ

saying? Most people that you go to, they won't be honest

with you. So I'm honest with you, you aren't right. Say, "I

have believed and thereafter be upright." So there is one

path allowed to us going up. You can't go up to heaven on

a crooked path. You can't go up to heaven with half-truths;

giving your heart to truth on one side, and pulled to the

side by a lie on the other side. You see! You've got to be

all right. You have got to be whole. You've got to take

your whole life up to G-d, not part of it – whole life. You

want to go up straight; you want to get to heaven, take

your whole life up to G-d. Your love for women, your love

for money, your love for truth and everything else, take it

straight up to G-d. Don't be crooked! So, it's the straight

way up, mustaqeem – straight up, as those youngsters say

on the street – straight up – mustaqeem!

Now, only one path up, but the soul that's speaking in the

Qur'an and confessing to G-d, that we weren't able to

Imam W. Deen Mohammed

come by all these paths without your guidance; your guidance has made it possible for us to come to our subulumaa – many paths. So the paths going horizontal are many. What are they? We should begin with the sciences. These parts are astronomy, mathematics, geography and all the other sciences we have. They are innumerable – we can't number all of them – so many divisions of science or disciplines. Say, disciplines of science and each science in itself will have its discipline and in all of them together, represent independent or major disciplines that are connected by relationship to one another in the total scheme or the total system of matter. They are connected.

So, these are subulumaa. Subul is a plural of sabeel. So subul; these are the paths going like this, and they are many. But then Allah gives us also one down here, doesn't he. Now there are many paths – the disciplines of the many sciences that are paths and why are they are paths on the vertical? Because they never start moving until we reach another person with them. If I got some science, I know, I discover some science, it won't move in the world until I reach another person with it. When I reach another person with it, then it starts to move. That's why they are horizontal; they're going from person to person. But there is a nature in me. There's a thirst and hunger in my soul that wants to connect with its maker, his creator, who's responsible for my existence being here. Who started my life in the creation and it wants to connect with my G-d. It goes straight up. I don't have to talk to you, in fact if I talk to you, I get off track. G-d says there is nothing between him and the seeker who seeks him, not even a thin veil. So we go straight up to our G-d and we see this beautiful universe. We find him. Say, this is too much for my mind to digest, too much for my eyes to totally comprehend. So it humbles the soul. It humbles the ego. It humbles the intellect, the mind. The mind falls down. When Moses saw a little piece of the reality, he fainted – and his tongue was tied, too. Maybe Aaron wouldn't have fainted but his eyes certainly would have been opened. So, we know when we see the bigger reality, we humble ourselves. Any intelligent, intellect, mind humbles itself; and then you find not only your own reality (see when man comes to the conclusion that my reality has limitation, my reality is not the big reality; there's a bigger reality than mine. When he comes to that reality, he really sees himself). You know, most of us can't make headway; we can't be successful in this life because we have an exaggerated picture of our own selves. We have an exaggerated picture of our own worth and Hollywood is making us think now that we can get shot and get back up. We can be dropped from the empire state building and keep running. Isn't that what they have pictures doing – pictures of human beings just walking, running on air, running through the space. Jump from a high tower or something, hit the ground and roll over and keep going; just hoping that a lot of our ignorant children will believe that can happen (and believe me, some of them are going to believe that can happen). And that's another way of dropping dead weight. The world is too heavy with dead weight, so the world wants to drop a lot of dead weight. Just like the plane, it says, well this storm is rough. We're going to have to throw something off. They throw all the baggage off and they say something else has got to go off. They look and see who's from the ghetto, who's not needed so much in our world and they start dropping off. Well, that's just the way this culture is doing. This culture is dropping off dead weight, and they're designing it to do that. It's criminal, yes it is. Yes! So these are the paths, but G-d says, "Take you one path, of these many, for my sake." You may follow the path of physics and devote yourself to physics as a professor, as a

scientist or whatever, and it may just occupy all your time
and your interest, right? You haven't got time for anything
else. Well, you have come up on a path that's productive
alright, and that's useful to mankind alright, but you have
allowed yourself to be taken from G-d. So G-d wants us to
know that he made all of these paths for us. "I made all
these paths for you, but choose you one over all the rest"
so he says, "spend in the way of G-d, in the path of G-d,
with your wealth and with your own souls." Spend in the
path of G-d. This is the horizontal way.

And what did the Prophet ﷺ say? The Prophet ﷺ
said, cautioning us on how to give, he says, "don't spend
so heavily or so much that you extend your arm out to the
furthest extent." That means that you give all. You put
your arm out the farthest as it can go. That means you gave
up all you have and he says, "don't hold it so close to your
neck that you become guilty of being stingy." A hoarder of
wealth; he said don't put it so close and don't put it so far.

Now, you notice, some crosses of Christianity, they're
long, long like that, but a lot of them are like this. Well,

those reflect intelligence; that are short like this and reflect a just world – the world not asking (all that the people have). You go somewhere and they got a big old cross. I saw one on the highway – a big old cross, way out here. I think it was on highway 57, a big old cross that goes way out there like that. So whoever those people are, they're saying, "we want everything you got. Give it all up!" So when we understand these signs, we can understand our Prophet better.

Obviously, our Prophet was taught to read, not only the Qur'an, he was taught to read the universe and he read everything that man writes in secret. And it said in the Qur'an, "Say, no he wasn't there when you all were having your secret council." How does he know these things? Did he sneak in here or is he standing on the other side of the door or something, listening. G-d says, "No, he wasn't there when you were holding your secret council." Well, how does he know our secrets, how did he get all of our secrets. Says, "G-d is knower of whatever is in the heavens and whatever is in the earth. He is knower of both that's published and that that is kept secret. He is knower of the seen and the unseen, etc."

So, the sabil — we're going to take off subul which means
many paths going horizontal, or this way. And we're going
to put sabil, the path of G-d. Subul belongs to G-d, too, but
we say sabil-Allah, the one that belongs to G-d. Spend in
this one with your wealth and with your own souls. You
know how to spend with your wealth, that doesn't need
any understanding, but how do I spend with my own soul?
Your own soul is supposed to know truth. Your own soul
is supposed to know when it hears truth. Well, when you
know truth, don't keep it to yourself. Share it with others
who need the truth. You don't have to have money. You
don't have to have U.S. dollars or anybody else's dollars to
spend in the way of G-d. You have the truth; share it with
others who need the truth. You have love; share it with
others who need love, Praise be to Allah! So this is
spending in the path of G-d, not just with money, but with
your own souls. Spend with your own souls.

Let's take the cross off, that looks like the cross Peter was
hung on. Yes, they say he was hung upside down – Peter,
and he remained the root. He remained the head of the
church – even till now, hanging upside down. I think

they're kind of repenting…. having a mouth, eating what the earth produced and get the feet (you and me who follow the religious up in the sky), feet up in the sky, head down under, chewing up everything the poor people have; and others too if they will give it to them – just eating it up. I think the church is repenting that. The church was like that for most of its life. You know that. It gathered wealth; that's why they were able to stay in power so long. They gathered great wealth and treated the masses like animals; like they were nothing but animals – nice little animals. They have to take care of their animal and if you gave them trouble, they abandoned you. This was the old order. And, not that it didn't do any good – it did a lot of good. Some of them even developed the sciences and advanced sciences, but on the whole, they hoarded the wealth; they gathered the wealth and hoarded it and deprived the public – their public of a good life until Martin Luther and Protestantism – the change came and mind you, that was after Mohammed, the Prophet ﷺ had done his work on this earth. Long after, then they finally came and made things better; much better.

So we begin by saying Allah identifies Mohammed ﷺ in the Qur'an. He, himself, G-d himself shows us

Mohammed ﷺ – identifies him for us to see and

understand him. And he is firstly, a mercy to all the worlds

and he's also a liberator. He liberates those who are

unjustly burdened and believe me that was all souls on this

planet earth. Falsehood, false perception in religion

burdens everyone who accepts it. So, actually, he comes to

lift the burdens from the backs, the yoke, or the heavy

weight that sits way down on the backs from all people,

not just us. So that's why it says he's a mercy for all the

worlds, and also it says that he is a mercy for all people

and then we come to see him as a mercy and a liberator, a

comforter. The Bible says there's a comforter coming. A

comforter will come after Jesus Christ and that one is

addressed as 'another;' didn't say the same; and will send

you another comforter. This is the Bible, Gospel, New

Testament. The world will be sent another comforter. It's a

shame that many in the Muslim world believe that Jesus

Christ is coming back. They don't understand that

Mohammed ﷺ is the true Jesus Christ, he is the true

Jesus Christ. Mohammed ﷺ wasn't the kind of man to

want to make himself be seen. He's not that kind of man.

He refused that. He wouldn't even accept it, but

بسم الله الرحمن الرحيم

Imam W. Deen Mohammed

Mohammed ﷺ is the true Jesus Christ. The Jesus Christ

that we have in the Bible points to Mohammed ﷺ. He is

the sign, pointing to the reality. Jesus Christ of the Gospel

is only the sign pointing to the reality, Mohammed the

Prophet ﷺ.

Now, that's something that most leaders won't tell you; I
mean in Islam. They won't tell you that. They have us all
spooked up; have us confused. We can't even get the
benefit, the full benefit of the religion that we believed in
and accepted, we can't get it because they are mystifying
the truth so much and confusing our minds so much, we're
wondering, well who is the last Prophet? If you're waiting
on Jesus Christ, he's come, Mohammed's ﷺ come. So,
looks like Jesus Christ is going to be the last Prophet. Are
you saying he's G-d? Are you agreeing with Christians,
he's G-d? He's got to come back? Is he going to be G-d?
Is he a Prophet? What is he going to be? Coming back?

Mohammed ﷺ already came and he said it is finished.

He concluded it, the last Prophet. Now, why is he coming behind; he had to come back? The dead has to arise; I agree with that, the dead have to rise. But whatever they're talking about, we're already back and when we came up out of the grave, when we broke the ground, and came up into the light of freedom, justice and equality, we saw Mohammed ﷺ. We didn't see a Jew. So we want to tell those Sheiks and Imams and what all else they are, we want to tell them that they've got it wrong! And if they want to break crosses and wait for Jesus Christ to come back; help yourself! We're going to get the farthest away from you as we can, because we know that where you are in hell. They are in hell and don't know it and the Christians, with intelligence in the high leadership, they look down on the Islamic world and they say, "aren't they pitiful? They don't even understand their own Prophet!" Praise be to Allah.

So we come now to Mohammed, the Prophet ﷺ and business. How should we connect him with business? Well, he was a businessman before Allah revealed to him the Qur'an and Allah said to him, (the first word Allah spoke to him) was read and Allah said to him "read!" And we think it meant read the Qur'an; the Qur'an wasn't spoken yet. He just gave one word, "read!" Now we know read is followed by the Iqrah, "read in the name of your lord who created." Iqrah – again. He didn't say Allah, he didn't say even his name, but he gave an attribute of his. So, he gave the attribute, "the creator" and how does revelation begin in the Bible, giving us G-d as the creator. Is that not true? He is one who created all that existed, all that's on earth and in the heavens. He is the creator of all things.

That's how G-d is introduced in genesis, the beginning of the Bible, as the creator and later he gets those other attributes – the other attributes are introduced later, but first, the creator; and introduced as the creator, the process of creation is put in the picture – is put before our eyes in a picture. There was void, everything was void; there was nothing existing and the spirit moved along the face of the waters. Well, nothing was existing – but all of a sudden, like a dream, water pops into the picture and then a spirit moving along the surface of that water pops into the

___

picture. And there was darkness upon the deep and G-d says, "Let there be light, and there was light." Where was the light? In the deep! And that light came from the depths and ended up filling the whole world with light. Eventually, there was a moon up and a sun up, and all the star's and everything else, and it keeps multiplying until we see a whole created world. Right?

So, it's saying, the world came out of darkness. What is this addressing? Education! This is addressing the teaching or the education of the human mind and soul because when you educate the human mind, you educate the human soul. The soul becomes wise because the mind has digested the true knowledge.

G-d says, "Read" to him and a lot of us think it means he gave him the Quran. He meant read the Quran. Yes, he meant that, but he meant more than that. He meant read the universe. How do we know? G-d says, "in that, that is above you, there are signs; and that, that is below (meaning on earth) there are signs and as well as your own self and the human creation, too, there are signs." And the same word that's used for the ayats in the Qur'an is a word

used in that language. It says ayats, so the Qur'an, the
language, the reading, is in the form of verses or what we
call ayats, making up chapters, etc. Ayats, verses. But we
say verses, but actually ayat is signs; means literally signs.
So, the language of the Qur'an is composed of signs and
its character is signs. The character is signs but likewise is
the whole reality, everything, including our own selves.
When we look at ourselves, we see that. So, this is the
powerful, powerful message. So what is this saying, and
obviously there was those in the hearing range of the

Prophet Mohammed ﷺ. There was those who

understood the deep meaning and the beauty of the Qur'an
when he was giving it to them. They understood it. There
was those blessed to see it as there are those blessed to see
right here. There are those right before me right now; you
see and understand, and you're saying hurry up Imam, we
understand this. But I have to slow up. I got a donkey back
there and he can't see that heavy weight on his back, you
know.

He can't see Hollywood, the whole Hollywood has been
shrunk in to a dense package, and it weighs a few million
pounds, and he's carrying it right behind, but he doesn't

know he's carrying it. So G-d meant for him to read creation, that's why he introduced himself as creator, to connect himself with the objective world; the world of matter. And when he said to Mohammed ﷺ, read, it was

because he was going to connect Mohammed ﷺ with the world of matter. He said, "Read in the name of your lord who created." The first read didn't help him. The second read didn't help him, but when he connected himself as creator with the command to read, Mohammed

ﷺ understood that. Mohammed ﷺ was a man of great intelligence and common sense. So when G-d says, "connect me with my world that I've made, with whatever is in the sky, and whatever is in the earth and with your own life, with your own self. And now I'm saying, read".

Mohammed ﷺ said, "He means for me to read what's in creation. To read what's in myself? In other words, study yourself and learn how to read what you learn from your own self. Study this creation of mine and learn how to read what you discover in my creation. That's an invitation to liberate the human being with universal knowledge and sciences.

Imam W. Deen Mohammed

This is an education process that G-d is creating or bringing about. And he says that he created man and then he said, "Another creation." Created him once, then he said, "Another creation." Create again, and then he says in the Qur'an, "the merciful G-d taught the Qur'an. Then he said, "And created the human person." So this is telling us how the next man is created or how the higher man is created. The higher man is created by teaching him the revelation or revealed truth from G-d, then it goes into him and he becomes another creation or a new creation. And Allah said, "That he is the one who gave you the life as you see it now;" the beautiful things that grow out of the earth – the cultural life that comes straight from the natural world that G-d made. Said, "He's the one who gives you that." Say, "But he promises you another rising of the culture." Another birth of even the culture; so there is the natural culture and then G-d promises there will be a second rising or a second birth of culture. And when will that come? That will come after he create the man over with the knowledge he inspires. And the man will have a new world, a new culture. Isn't that wonderful?

Now, I'm not buying the culture of the Islamic world, no!
Let us have it in America, in the USA from where
something is starting real big right here; yes! He is creating
us all over again. He's making a new people. And look
how he decided to have these new people. In his wisdom,
that's a mystery to us! We cannot understand his wisdom
always. It's a mystery to us. We understand so much, but
much of it is a mystery. How he would let a people fall
into the hands of cruel people – a people that were already
conquered in their own homeland. They were conquered
by warring factions who found that they could make
money off of them, selling them to the people who would
come to the new world where labor was needed. And then
he allowed that these people, these souls that were
conquered in their own land and sold to traders, who
traded in tea and other merchandise, but also in human
merchandise – traded in slaves that they'll be sold. They're
sold here and have their human classifications degraded
where they're no more considered full humans, but two
thirds of a man. That he permit all that. Permit the
innocent to be lynched and burned – at the stake; in the
history of this country, he permits all of that; permits that a
whole people be put down by the world; not just America.
I heard nobody in Egypt stand up and say, "They're not

115

sub-human, they're not two-thirds human." I didn't hear anybody from Mecca stand up and tell the world, "hey, you've got human beings over there, and you're saying they're two-thirds human; they're not two-thirds human, they're all human just like you are." Nobody came to our rescue! Until a stranger came who was a victim in his country of the same kind of racism that we were the victims of in our country; so he came sharing our feelings, and sharing our hope, and he came and he set off some powerful dynamite – the blackest powder this world has ever seen, and it blew up in the heart of the land and threw up a mountain a mile high.

And he said, Elijah may not be able to get to the top of that mountain, but if Elijah helps his son like I obligated him to, Wallace is going to get to the top of that mountain and thank G-d, I got to the top of that mountain. Al-hamdu-lillahi-Rabbil-alamin! Yes, I got to the top of that mountain. Oh, yes! Well, you know everything has happened that he was going to do. A shortage in gravity, uncontrollable fire; burning for three hundred ninety years, and all that you know. And I'm here now to stop the pollution, clear the air. Praise be to Allah!

Yes, so how are we to see him then? As an individual? We know he was upright and a perfect human character before he received any word of revelation. He was that. He had that honorable life established for himself, among his countrymen and they said, "He is the truthful" and they said, "he does not tell a lie and they said he is El-Amin; he does not break the trust. If you trust him, he delivers. That's what they knew of him before G-d spoke one word, "read" to him. He was already established in that mold, or in that excellence, and after he became leader. Now understand this, we mentioned this today in conversation. It was mentioned how he swept floors for his wife and that the beauty of that picture is not just seeing a man sweeping floor, but to know the works of the man who was sweeping the floors. That this man is a statesman, he's the head of his people, he's the head of the country. He runs affairs and they, all of them, turn to him for guidance. All the people of the land, big and small, look to him for guidance, so when you see a man in that big picture, and he's sweeping the floors, now you can see why it's important to keep in history, to put him in history as a person who swept the floors for his wife. I said yes, that's right, because if you see one of us sweeping the floor for our wife, it's probably because we don't have a job, and we're trying to give her something. We can't give her much, but I'll sweep the floors today, sweetheart. So Allah says of him, "he is a mercy to all the worlds." And if you understand it deeper, "he is a mercy to all systems of knowledge." He is going to relieve the burden that's on the human intellect; going to liberate the human intellect by connecting the human intellect with the objective world and giving that human intellect the message from G-d; that He has created that objective world for the curious mind of all of His servants. For the curious minds of all of His creatures, all of His human creation – that He has created us to engage the world with our intelligence and our hearts, not just our mind – our intelligence and our hearts. It first has to be in the hearts. The thinker, the free thinker; he became a free thinker because the world was too much of a burden on his mind and heart, just like Mohammed ﷺ did. He left his own people, and went up in the mountain because the condition of his people was too much of a burden on his heart and mind. So he went up into the mountain to seek relief and to find truth. So this is the free thinker.

The free thinker sees the miseries of the human lot and he goes off to himself, away from everything, so that he'll be free to think on his own and find truth and he hopes. G-d has his will in every human being, you know that? We may be asleep to it, be unconscious of it, but his will is in every human being. And once you start straining for that, that G-d knows will help, not only you, but will help mankind; G-d gives you assistance from His own will and you may not know it at the time, you don't recognize that G-d is with you, you aren't working by yourself. But finally one day with G-d's favor on you, you will realize that all the time you were working, G-d was your co-pilot. He was working right with you all the time. So,

Mohammed ﷺ comes as a comforter. Jesus comforted the people as a sign. They had faith. That's why you come to Jesus by faith. You come to Jesus by faith. Believe in him and that's all you have to do. Why? Because he is a hope, he's a promise, pointing to the world to come that's going to be right and just; the kingdom of G-d. A better reality, a better existence; so he is the pointer, pointing to that – if you have faith in him and hold fast and remain steadfast; eventually you're going to live to see the second

119

comforter, "and I shall send you another comforter." This is the Bible. So if you hold on you will get the second comforter.

Now, we were holding on to Mr. Fard, a sign pointing to the next one. And if we were listening to the Hon. Elijah Muhammad, you know there would be a next one because he said, "this one will not live forever. After him there would be another one." And he said, "The next one may accept some of what this one has and he might reject all of it." That's what I heard the Hon. Elijah Muhammad say with these ears; I heard him say that. So, you know the Hon. Elijah Muhammad said many things that made us think that Mr. Fard is the end and he will always be god. No! He gave us a belief in a man that was to be temporarily our god. Maybe he will survive some generations, but there will come a time when our children will still be here and they will have no Mr. Fard as god. That's the teachings of the Hon. Elijah Muhammad, and he said, "The next one that comes, he might take some of, or keep some of what Mr. Fard had, and he might reject it all. He said he might reject it all.

Now, have I rejected all of it? No, but are you god? No! I'm not god and certainly Mr. Fard wasn't god either. We're nothing but human beings, trying to help ourselves first, and then our brothers get on the right path. That's all we are. But you know Jesus Christ, he found a man that couldn't see (blind) and if you had seen what he did to that blind man's eyes you would think he was very cruel. Now, the man already can't see, then he took mud and put mud over the man's eyes. That's just like burying his eyes isn't it? But he buried his eyes in a deeper darkness so that he would strain harder to see. Fard did the same thing. He buried our brains in the urge in the brain to know the truth. He put more dead matter on it and buried it; put in deep in the ground (I guess he went six feet deep), I think we were only two feet deep, then he pushed our brain back down in the earth six feet deep so we would strain harder to see. And just like Jesus Christ brought sight to the blind man by putting mud on his eyes, Mr. Fard brought sight to the blind man by putting mud on our eyes. Yes, putting mud on our eyes. You know mud is solid earth or solid soil, or ground, with too much water to support life. Most plants won't grow in mud. Maybe, rice will. There are some things that will grow in mud, like rice and a few other things, but most things won't grow in mud. You sure can't

grow a tree in mud, you'll kill it. Yes, you'll kill the tree if
you keep the ground that it's in muddy. It will die; can't
live in mud – can't get roots, can't live in mud. And you
know what we were called up until I was about thirteen or
fourteen years old? Yeah, Wallace Muckmud, Wallace D.
Muckmud, W. D. Muckmud – all of my family members;
Muckmud – my father, Elijah Muckmud. One Imam, no,
minister (I tend to say Imam because that's the language
now); Sulton, Minister of Milwaukee originally. My
father gave him a little more, bigger work to do and he
went out to other cities and states (Sultan) and he would
begin his talk in the temple. He would say, "What is your
name Mr. Black man," and he would give examples;
Johnny Washington and stuff like that. "Where did you get
that name from? That's the name of your slave master. My
name is Sultan Muckmud!" I heard him as a child. I know
– I am not copying somebody else. I'm giving you the
sound I heard from his mouth, ok! Sultan Muckmud he'd
say! Well, the Bible speaks about the muck and the mud,
yes, it does. That language is in the Bible – muck and mud.
You can't have life in muck and mud. But Mr. Fard comes
behind him and says, "Yeah you have put their senses in
muck and mud, but when I get through with them, you
going to see that you have not killed them, they're going to

rise again." Yes! And you know he made it clear what his role was. He called us, "the mentally dead – how to resurrect, give life to the mentally dead." I'm only sharing that with you all because some of you right here with me today, you remember that. You know about that and your intention is good, your faith is strong and your hearts are right, and Allah has saved you for a great, great time.

So I conclude with Mohammed ﷺ, as a person, who was guided by G-d to read the system, the language and systems of his creation and pass that knowledge on to the hungry, thirsting minds or intellects of the people of his time - those who were in his immediate company, the people of Arabia, but he also reached out to Persia (called Iran now), and to Egypt and Ethiopia through Bilal and those Ethiopians that later came to know about his mission during his lifetime – and even to Europe. All the way to Europe; he reached all the way to Europe in his lifetime. He reached the intellects that far away - and thanks to Allah giving him to us in the world that we really can benefit from Qur'an and really have Mohammed's ﷺ life and his light with us at the same time. Not only the

Qur'an, we can have both the Qur'an and the light of
Mohammed ﷺ who's the guide for us understanding the
Qur'an and living the Qur'an as Allah intends. The creator
intends for us to live it. We have that – and we should see
him, not just as a businessman, but we should see him as
one that G-d gave mankind to lead us to global economics
– a one world system that will be just and reach all people
and give all people an opportunity to grow in the reality
that Allah created for all of us.

This is the time and it's going to improve and these bad
leaders who are selfish, who are getting in position over us
with our votes; and they really got in that position because
they wanted to get there so that they'll be able to serve
their private interests and they used us and the power we
gave them to serve their private interest. Don't worry,
don't let that burden you. Allah says, "I am a worker!" So
you work in your places. G-d is working all the time;
creating new universes out there and also supporting life
that needs his help everywhere. Yes, he is! So you be a
worker in your places! All of you shouldn't want to be
Imam W. Deen Mohammed. Some of you all should want
to be the producer who's providing us with the household

needs. With the garments and things and the clothing and the furniture and the appliances and things we need in our house. And some of us should be wanting to establish a financial system that will be owned by us and will help serve our financial needs. There are many, many, many, many avenues. So let us not neglect the many (sabil) that we have, but let us all see the sabilullah as that path on the horizontal plan that will save us from self-destruction, if we give our hearts too much to these private engagements or to this private interest.

Let us stay on the path of G-d while working in our places and working the things that we know how to work. Work those things and produce. We want to see great production. I don't know what Mr. Fard had in his mind when he called us the fruit of Islam, but brothers, in the new light that I see and understand and walk by now, we can really be the fruit of Islam for the whole world.

The Quran & Mohammed ﷺ

The Last Prophet

Jumuah - 9-1-2000

We thank Allah for our life. To him we give worship only and make complete submission; surrender our whole life and everything in our possession or authority to our G-d who made us, who created us and created everything and made it possible for us to have the things we have from his creation. Allah, most high, says in the Qur'an that he gives the human being their needs, their provisions, from the heavens and the earth. The sunshine, we couldn't live without it – it comes from above. The rain, we couldn't live without it, it comes from above and many other things come from above, but the most important things that he gives us from above, that gives us life like the rain – spiritual life! After we have been dead spiritually, it's his word, his revelation that descended in the night of power to Mohammed, the Prophet ﷺ; and we have it with us today; the Qur'an, the holy book of G-d, His book, the guidance to us and a purifier to cleanse our souls and our minds and our society – even the environment – of those things that are forbidden, the haram. And haram also is shirk, associating others as G-d, with G-d. Indeed, that is the worst form of oppression. The worst form of oppression, to put false gods over people.

Imam W. Deen Mohammed

We're living in a day and time that needs, more than ever, religion, true religion, straight religion, honest, sincere religion. We need it now more than ever. Why? As I see it, it is because what the word of G-d came to mankind or to the world of human beings, to prepare them for, is now here. Scripture came to Prophets thousands of years ago, and who knows, maybe twenty thousand years ago; maybe even longer, much further back than that. Allah says in his book, the Qur'an, he says, "that there has never been a nation that did not receive a messenger of G-d." G-d sent all of them warners, the word is warners! So, there has never been a nation without a warner coming to it. Then that means the oldest records of any nation that they can find, tells us that there was a messenger back then, too. Not only a nation, but a messenger had come to them at one time or another in their life.

We think of the Bible as a book of prophecy, because it contains a lot of prophesy, but it also contains a lot of history and it contains a lot of stories, like the Qur'an, but much more the Quran. The Qur'an is a condensed book. In the Qur'an it says it's written, "And they are astonished, they're amazed, that this book leaves no matter out, neither small nor large." Whatever has been revealed before is dealt with in the Qur'an. Neither big matters nor small matters are left out of the Qur'an. The Qur'an addressed them all.

We hear many things as Muslims from the teachers, the Imams, from myself giving the khutbah, and many of us think that what we're hearing is only from the Qur'an – only from Mohammed ﷺ, from Islam; not necessarily so. I would say, if most of what we give is not already given before in some other holy book, or some other scripture, we're not giving the truth, because the Qur'an is a treatment of scriptures that came before and an explanation and a completion! I'm giving you the words of G-d, not my words. This is what the Qur'an is.

There's religions that don't have the idea of G-d that we have in religion like Judaism, Christianity, Islam, even Sabians religions that's mentioned in the Qur'an. These religions have similar designs, similar constructions, similar language, especially when we're trying to address

Imam W. Deen Mohammed

G-d and what G-d is and who G-d is, and trying to address man, human beings, what the human beings family is and what our purpose in on this earth. These religions are all similar, very similar.

The other religions, like Buddhism, Hinduism and there are many more, they don't claim to believe in a G-d like we believe in a G-d. Hinduism is filled with gods, as you know. There are many gods. Buddhism, they claim that they don't have a god. There's no god. Buddha is an enlightener; he comes to enlighten mankind, to educate mankind. He's not a god they say. That's what the Buddhist say (not what some books that are written in the west – over here by us, or by some westerner), but what they say. I've had occasions in the last five years of my life to meet with some of the most learned Buddhists on this earth and I've learned from them things I didn't know about their religion. Hearing from them, I'm convinced that they do have a god. They just don't have a language for it. They have a god and the human being cannot exist without a god. Each and every one of you here, before you came to Islam, you had a god. And I'm not talking about what Christianity gave you. Even before you went to

130

Mohammed The Prophet ﷺ | The Perfect Man - The Complete Man

church you had a god. Man cannot exist without, a suspicion that, there is a power over him; that there is a higher power, authority over him. He can't exist without that. Now he may give a different description, but we all feel the same thing in our souls. So we all have gods, but our minds, our own reasoning without G-d's guidance gives us false G-ds, and this is the history of mankind; the history of human life on this earth.

Having this spirit inside and trying to give a description to what we sense in our souls, and we do it with our own minds over the history, and many thousand years of human history, we can see how this human family have evolved and has come into a rational belief a rational religion – a rational faith. Early attempts to establish a religion may show nothing but guess work, fear, superstition. It shows only what has been in the dream of those people. In their dreams, in their nightmares, in their troubled times when they were fearing the storms would wipe their village away forever, or the drought would never end and they would all die, or when they planted the crops and put all their sweat and blood into it and were hoping for a big yield at the end of the season when harvest time comes.

131

And they strained to pray to a power outside of
themselves, bigger than themselves, that they believed
could answer their prayers and what they came up with
was their own religion, not necessarily humanity's
religion, but these other religions that I named that are
kindred religions, (the religion of the Sabians, the Jews,
the Christians and the Muslims). These religions - they are
religions for humanity; not necessarily for tribes, or a
segment of this population on this earth of human beings,
but for the whole humanity. Those religions are truly
revealed religions. And as I said, even in ancient times, if
there were nations on this earth building roads as we are
told in history, houses and fortresses, etc. and having trade
on the high seas, in ancient times, many thousands of years
ago, they must have, according to Qur'an, we must, I
would say, also accept that they had messengers come to
them. That means, if messengers came to them from G-d,
the messengers came to them to advance the knowledge of
the religion of humanity. See, there's a difference between
religious and religion. One is religion of humanity. The
other is imagination.

As Allah put it in the Qur'an "only guessing and
imagining." G-d inspired the seekers to seek what is there
for his human existence; not for his African existence, not
for his European existence – for his human existence. And
we have lived, no, we're blessed to be living in the end of
time for this progression. By progression, I mean this
continuous effort over the thousands and thousands of
years to inform man of his own reality and how he is made
and given that reality by his Lord; the G-d, the creator of
everything. To advance that knowledge in mankind has
been going on for thousands of years and now we have
lived to see the conclusion of that. This is a wonderful
time. It actually concluded as revelation, fourteen centuries
or so ago when Mohammed ﷺ received, in the night of
power, the first words of G-d to him for mankind, now, the
Qur'an in its completed script. Wonderful!

People say, "Oh, why should I believe in G-d?" If you're
educated in religion, you would never ask that question. If
you're educated in religion you could easily answer that
question for anybody. Why should I believe in G-d?
Because G-d's word has proved true against all other
words! G-d's authority has prevailed over all other

authorities! And the world today looks exactly like the Prophet ﷺ said it would look fourteen hundred years ago! It looks just like they said it will look. G-d told them how it would look in the end and that's exactly the way it looks – just like they described it. That's why you should believe in G-d – if you have no other reason! But if you're an honest human being you should believe in G-d because you have nothing else to help you, except G-d when you get in serious trouble. Every human being knows that. When we were slaves we knew the white master that enslaved us, we knew he wasn't going to answer our prayers. We forgot the name Allah, Jehovah, whatever – we had forgotten all that. But we learned from them, the English word G-d, and we called on G-d. See, we need a language, some language. If you don't have one, you will form one of your own. You're a human being – intelligent, inventive; praise be to Allah.

If you knew how I felt now, you would feel a hundred times better than you feel now. Only my lord knows how I feel now. I'm seeing, as I'm talking to you, the reality, and it makes me want to just be absolutely still. My mouth, my tongue, my limbs, even my heart beat wants to slow down.

It is something. You can't be ignorant and appreciate this to the extent that I do. G-d has made me wise. When I was in my early years, twenty's, thirty's, even the beginning maybe, in my forty's, I couldn't appreciate revelation, the Prophet ﷺ, and the human being inside in the excellent mold that G-d made him, like I do now. No way! As you become more educated, then you have a bigger picture of truth, therefore a bigger appreciation for truth. Never will all the people be equal in knowledge. G-d didn't make us like that. All of us will have knowledge, but never will all of us equal in knowledge. So, if we're never going to be equal in knowledge, then that means we're never going to be equal in our appreciation for this religion. You get the logic!

So, G-d has made mothers and fathers to take care and protect children and see them up to manhood or has prepared them for the challenges of this world. And G-d has made Prophets and messengers and religious teachers, who are under those Prophet and messengers, the guardians of the faith. And we have to appreciate good (this is not for me, I'm out of the picture. I don't see myself when I'm talking like this). We have to make our proven leaders, who have proven their virtues to us; who have proven that they're virtuous people. First, that they're faithful people. They'll have faith in G-d; they're faithful people and they're virtuous people, and they are studious people, they study and are compassionate people and generous people. We have to support them as our leaders and you sit before them like you're sitting before me now, most of you. Allah has blessed me also with good people to support me. You sit before them, and you listen attentively and you don't go looking for something to condemn. You'll be looking for something to support your life and help you with the job of living on this earth with your relatives, with your neighbors, with the world – be listening for that. Don't listen for something to increase your doubts. Listen for something to increase your faith and you'll be successful, and we'll have a great community. We'll have great communities if the people of faith would do that. Yes, great communities.

It's nothing new. Human life is nothing new, it's the same. It's the same as it was six thousand years ago, or four thousand years ago, or eight thousand years ago. It hasn't changed. Human life is the same. There are two types of human beings. One is the human being that feels indebted and because of feeling indebted, wants to help somebody else, wants to do something for somebody. Then there is the other kind of human being. That human being does not feel indebted and want to get something from somebody else, wants to get. That's the truth. G-d calls it what, "those who are ungrateful." The ungrateful and the grateful; that's how he separates them.

The ungrateful, they are in degrees, and the worst of them is the Satan, the Shaitan himself. He is the most ungrateful of all creatures – Satan, Shaitan in Islam. Satan, the most ungrateful of all the creatures; and he depends on the ungrateful to support him and his design on the world – his plan for the world. So, he's constantly working on those who have weak faith to get them to throw out all faith and become ungrateful. Then he can use them. They're his then. They're with the devil. Well, in our religion, we are told of the end of days. That language sounded more like Bible doesn't it. Yes! The last days, the end of days, we're told of the conclusion of things, that this world, all of it, has been formed upon a logic and a law and this universal logic and these universal laws that expresses its logic in

137

different branches, in different forms – it's cherished by
the devil, the Satan, the Shaitan, who sees it as his tool, his
tool for putting him up as the god of mankind (now he's,
in his own thinking). He, in his own thinking, never sees
himself in this light. He never sees himself going against
the creator, G-d the true G-d who's the creator. There's no
other G-d except the creator. He sees himself as an aide, as
an agent, aiding G-d. He interprets G-d's law and the logic
for himself, and he thinks because he is able to perceive it,
to know it with his own mind and thinking that it's
intended for him. So the logic is his possession, he thinks.
Now G-d, since you made me of fire and you made me to
have this knowledge that I have, why don't you let me use
it. Why you make me for it, and don't let me use it? Why
are you going to give this human being, this goody, goody,
who doesn't know how to use falsehood and sin and
corruption to beat these dumb, stupid humans of yours into
submission so they will be ready for you, I'll get all of
them ready for you if you leave them to me. When I get
through with them, they'll be begging for you, they'll be
begging you to come into their life, but G-d says no. I do
not advance truth upon falsehood. So he cut him off; told
him no and rejected him and he was hurt so bad, he said,
"since you have disappointed me like this, that I'm going

out and I'm going to go to these humans from before their faces, from behind their backs, from their left and their right side and said, "when I have finished with them, you won't have any worthy of what you've given them except a very few, your elect." And G-d gave him that freedom. G-d created everything to be free. You say, "A stone isn't free." That's what you think. You think a stone isn't free. It may not be free to move about like you, but it's free. It hasn't got anybody dictating what it should do; you never see it trying to polish itself up. You have to polish it up yourself, don't you? Nobody dictates anything to it. It has nothing to expect of its life, except its life, its existence. That's what I mean by that.

Alright, now, before the world was made in our religion (and it's in the Bible, too if you know how to find it, how to identify it) it is said by our Prophet Mohammed ﷺ, the messenger of G-d, that G-d invited the arch angel Jibreel (Gabriel in Christian language) to come and see the great world that he was about to form. And he showed it to Gabriel. This is hadith, the reports collected by Bukhari or Muslim, and some others. It is reported that G-d showed the creation to Gabriel (Jibreel in Islam) and when Jibreel saw it, he said, "my lord, (you didn't know that Jibreel had a lord, too, did you? Yes. The Holy Ghost has a lord, too). He said, "my lord, how can anyone go wrong in such a wonderful world?" Then G-d showed him the same world that he was going to create after Satan had got into the picture and influenced the world and when Jibreel looked at it he said, "My lord, how can anyone go straight in such a world?" So that's telling us (that's really education, to educate us) that if it were not for Satan, everybody would have a good life. If it were not for Satan deceiving you out of your forms that G-d put you in, everybody would have a good life. And that's also saying that man is created good. You hear me, but if the tempter temps him out of his nature, his form (his original nature and his original form) that is responsible for him having the bad life that he has, Satan, the adversary, the enemy of all human beings. He's the enemy of all human beings. He doesn't want us to be the human that G-d made us to be. And prophecy, before and with the Qur'an, warns us of that plan of Satan to bring humanity down and prove mankind unworthy of this great intellect that G-d has created him with.; unworthy of it; this great tool that produced, out of the world (original world that G-d made) all of these beautiful worlds of art and science, etc. That man himself has created. So Satan, he wants to prove us unworthy of that freedom and that great station that G-d created us for in his creation. He wants to bring us down.

Now the end of the world. What do we expect the picture to look like in the end of the world? In the end of the world, according to the word of G-d, man will be so taxed, so heavily burdened with things to do. He'll be so busy with things to do and he won't have time to reflect, to do some moral thinking. So because of this, his mental energy being so overly taxed, being so fully and completely used up or occupied (his mind that is) he won't be in a situation to keep to moral life that an ignorant man in a normal situation can manage. So the devil will be making great strides. Satan, Shaitan will be making great strides. In the end of time, we expect to see the worst picture of corruption – the end of times much of what we hear as statements, seem to be statements in the past time, were not as much statements for the past times as those statements of revelation, were and are, for the present time. Corruption has spread over land and sea. This is in the Bible and also in the Qur'an. And crowds will be going hastily, moving hastily about and there will be a lot of noise. Now when these revelations were given, the world was very quiet, relatively speaking. In fact, it was silent almost, relatively speaking. It was silent, a very quiet world (the earth that is). So it's prophesying; its scripture is telling us that there is coming a time when man's life, man's society will be crowded and there will be a lot of noise. Don't look back there, look at today. There have never been crowds like we have today on this planet. And there has never been noise like we have on this planet today. So we are living in the time of the conclusion of the revelation. The revelation concluded as a communication to man from G-d (as I said earlier) a little better than fourteen centuries ago. But what the revelation came to tell us of that, saw it coming on this earth is being concluded now in our time. It was not in my grandfather's time, it was not even in my father's time, but it is in my time (and that's your time because we're all here together). In our time, we're seeing the end of the world. Now, I'm not pointing to the Hon. Elijah Muhammad to say today more than I told you he was twenty-five years ago. He's a man, not a Prophet, not an angel, just a man, but he's a man used by higher power, ok, not missioned by higher power – used by the higher power. And his people are people not missioned by the higher power, but used by the higher power. And because his race and him in the position that we're in, in the realities of this world, we are more conditioned to strain for truth than other people. We're more conditioned to strain for answers than other people. So our psychic energies are higher than other people, on the whole. Our psychic perception is greater than theirs on the whole. Yes! The Hon. Elijah Muhammad spoke things that have come true. He said when I'm finished, it will be the end. The Hon. Elijah Muhammad passed in nineteen seventy-seven – seventy five, pardon me. I don't know why I said seventy-seven – two years later. Yes I do! Because most things come to their conclusion in sevens, - not two sevens; maybe that's why that was working in the back of my mind. Yes! The Hon. Elijah Muhammad passed in the year nineteen seventy five and by the end of the seventies, the world was finished.

You're looking for the physical destruction of the world. That's not what scripture is about. Scripture is not about the physical destruction of the world. It comes to destroy what man did to the world. It doesn't come to destroy the original world that G-d made. There's nothing wrong with the sun and the moon as G-d made it. And hence, nothing is wrong with the earth as G-d made it, but the bad world that the man has made following the Satan of this earth – the bad world, the bad earth that man has made following the Satan, that's what has to be destroyed.

The Hon. Elijah Muhammad left us and within a few years of his passing, we could see the end of the world had come. The presidents of this land just didn't have the spirit and enthusiasm that they had in earlier times; in the earlier history of this nation – not even the enthusiasm that John F. Kennedy had or Lyndon B. Johnson had. The later presidents just seemed to have lost their enthusiasm, lost their light, lost their spirit and we got used to it now after having two or three of them. We think they're all right. They are all right; they're very good people for the times, but they don't have the vision and enthusiasm that presidents had before the Hon. Elijah Muhammad's passing.

Sin just went to its extremes. Everything, just everything came out; approval for anything, everything corrupt and wrong. It started long before the Hon. Elijah Muhammad passed and after the Hon. Elijah's passing the crowds, the public changed their whole mind and attitude toward obedience to a higher authority. They think it isn't serious. They came to think that this is not serious (G-d, obey G-d, believe in G-d – you're not serious are you, buddy?) I mean, this is alright, but, that's too much to think about!

Homosexuality! You're afraid to speak against it now, you're afraid you might be hated by everybody. You might become a bad guy if you say something against the homosexuals. Drugs came out of the black man's neighborhood, went in to the white man's neighborhood – came out of the poor people's life and went into the rich people's life. Came out of the fools lives and went into the learned people's lives. Drugs – all these things just went rampant. If that isn't a sign of the end of time, what is! And everybody wants to have more money than they know they can possibly earn. Everybody – no matter how dumb, how unskilled – wants to have a lot of money, got to have it, and don't want to admit that they are poor to anybody. You can't hardly find a person that will admit they are poor; only when they are at home by themselves. When they step out that door, they're trying to make you think they've got money, "oh, how much is that? I really wanted

that. Can you put it in the lay-a-way for me?" And they
know it will be there long after they're dead. They will
never legally get enough money to buy that thing. "Will
you put it in the lay-a-way for me? No, I don't have quite
enough to pay for it now. I'll come back." Don't want to
admit, "I don't have enough money to even be in your
store. I'm supposed to be on my block, buying what's
there, waiting for somebody to bring me something." Poor,
but don't want to admit it.

In our holy book, G-d says, "that Satan gets you and
threatens you with poverty." He gets you to do wrong, to
accept corruption and he threatens you with poverty –
make you afraid that being poor is going to finish you; all
poverty is too much of a burden to carry. "I just can't be
poor." If you can't be poor, you're going to steal right? So
if you're poor and you don't have the skills or the where
with all to earn it legally, then if you can't stand poverty,
you're going to steal, you're going to hit somebody in the
head and take their money. You're going to snatch an old
lady's purse or something. So, Satan, he comes in, in the
end of time and he lifts crime way up. The crime that was
really bad before and the people hear about it. They say,

"Oh that happened. When did that happen?" Oh, two months ago I read about it. "Oh, that's terrible." Now, the second ago, the minute ago, I heard about it and it's much bigger as a problem, crime has mushroomed and the Satan has done this; the Satan himself has done this. By taking your mind away from G-d by causing you to perceive G-d differently. So G-d now is just a buddy that you take seriously when you want to, but the rest of the time you call on, "my G-d! Oh, my G-d, I forgot my hat, my curling irons, girl. Can I borrow yours? My G-d, where did you get that, wow, girl, tell me where you got that piece. I'm going to go get me one Friday, soon as I get my money." My G-d, use my G-d like you know, just nothing. Use my G-d, nothing, and I hate it.

One time I was in the public, and a lady said, "My G-d". I said, "did you call me?.... and I knew she wouldn't forget that. I just wanted her to remember that she's not supposed to say that, like that. At home I tell my children. You can't stop it, it's just like a contagious disease or something. Once it gets out it spreads, it spreads through the family and everybody like an epidemic. That's what it is. It becomes an epidemic. I hear one calling "my G-d." I said,

"Look, my G-d too. Not just yours. I don't like the way you used it. I don't like the way you used the name G-d." You have to check your children, because Satan is trying to get them completely under his influences. See, you have to be battling him all the time.

Now, the end of time. In our holy book, all of these things that we're seeing now, the great crowds, the epidemic of corruption, sin, filth, perversion of the excellent nature that G-d gave us as human beings. All of this that we see now, was prophesied of before, long time ago. In fact, thousands of years ago. And the Quran comes to bring the prophecy clearer to us, so we may be able to, more easily, identify it when it comes. Yes, this is what G-d told us about. You can easily identify it. Another sign, poverty, you're threatened by poverty. You can't raise your children like you want too for many reasons. But also, you can't even buy for them like you want to. You want to buy according to the reality of your pocket, or your bank account, but you can't do that. And you don't want to hurt their feelings, because some of the other boys and girls their age have those things. Television makes the child believe every child got these. So you feel so bad, you will really go against your good business, or money management sense, your own budget sense, and you'll go buy that expensive two hundred and something dollar shoes for your teenage child. That's what Satan has done for us!

Now, G-d says, that Satan bid's you to do evil, to follow corruption, and he threatens you with poverty. But G-d, He invites you to forgiveness and His favors, His blessings. It's the two, G-d is showing us the two forces, that have power in your life. G-d, and the Shaitan, the devil, Satan. The Satan, he invites you to a corrupt life, and threatens you with poverty, and the G-d, He invites you to forgiveness and He offers you whatever you like. But not in the mind the devil gave you. Whatever you like in the mind G-d created for you. Yes!

And it means these things, nice clothes. This coat here, so nice it cost so much, I'm going to take it off. I got it in California, LA. See, it has weight to it, see there. Ninety degrees, you aren't supposed to wear a coat like that but that thing looked so good on the rack, it looked better than all of those thin ones I have. I wanted to show it off today, on Jumuah day. Oh, you should see it up close, the fabric just speaks to you, talks to you. And that's one I bought with my paycheck. Most of the clothes you see me in, somebody, one of the Imams, or somebody, gave it to me, or bought it for me. But that one there, that's my money. I paid for it. I can't blame anybody for spending that kind of money on that coat. I did it myself, and if G-d keeps on helping me to move up in righteousness, and obedience to him and get more help from you, I'm going to get another one. Two or three more like it. Yes! The followers of Satan, they're not supposed to have nice things. The followers of G-d are supposed to have nice things. Allah-u-Akbar, Allah-u-Akbar. We want to change this thing, the way it's supposed to be. We're going to keep working at it too. Praise be to Allah, yes.

So in concluding this, both books say the word of G-d never can be changed. The Quran and the Bible. The word of G-d can never be changed. Whatever G-d says, it's there, it's permanent, and you can't change it. No changing the word of G-d. And G-d says, "The word of G-d is fulfilled in truth and justice". So this is not just a statement to us people. This is a prophesy! It's a

statement and a prophesy. It's saying that the Satan came
into the picture, the rebellious jinn, who was leading the
angels in the heavens, refused to accept G-ds plan to bring
man up on the earth and put him in charge of his own
affairs, (under G-d of course). He was so jealous, that he
went out to destroy the possibility of man being successful
in this great creation and great plan that G-d gave him. So
the word being proved true means that injustice will be
working against justice, and that Satan will be advancing
this trend to have injustice defeat justice, and falsehood
will be working against truth, and Satan will be the master.

He will be the genius advancing that trend, to have
falsehood defeat truth. Not falsehood in scripture only.
Falsehood in your life, to make you false. To make you
false as a person. To make you false as a thinker. To make
you false as a family man. False! But G-d says, "That His
word is fulfilled in truth and justice." Now, His word is
just not one word. His word is the whole book, the Quran.
It's a book of many words, but it's also called, "the word of
G-d", singular, for G-d gives us many words for our own
minds and needs, but with G-d, the whole message is as a
single word. Isn't this wonderful? That is wonderful, and

I would go so far as to tell you that, that single word is, "Mohammed's ﷺ obedience to Allah". That single word is the uswa of Mohammed ﷺ, his model for all who believe in G-d and fear the last day. That is one word, but it is revealed in all of these many words printed in the scripture to us as guidance to the mind of man. But with G-d, its only one word.

And that brings me to this point. The disbelievers who follow the influences of the Satan, the Shaitan, they want man to think that he's really created to be as bad as he is. He's really created to be as false as he is, that really, the human being is just a bad creation. Now, isn't that what art has said in many of its writings. Art, western art and perhaps some other art too; that man is just a bad creation. Look what one of the so-called philosopher poets said "to err (that means to make mistakes) is human, to forgive is divine." That statement to me is a statement coming out of the mouth of an innocent philosopher poet, but it was put into the mind and mouth of that poet by Satan himself. Now listen to it. Just listen to it. "To err is human, to forgive is divine." Forgiveness is a virtue, so what is he saying? Is he saying virtues are not of human nature, that human beings are not really a creature of virtues, that if he takes on virtues, he's taking on something that is not really of himself, something that's not of himself but is of G-d. So I have nothing but one choice then, be corrupt, or be G-d. Is that what he's saying, be corrupt or be G-d? You have no other choice because your virtues are not your own, but your ignorance, your flaws, your defects, your errors, those are yours. That's human! But truthfulness, like forgiveness, is divine. That's not yours!

And if you read scripture, if you understand scripture, if you recall scripture, or if you will read it for yourself, (if you have that interest) you'll find that these things have already been predicted, they have been told to us in scripture, that there is an effort to put man down, to put his worth down, to degrade him, to prove him to be unworthy of the value we usually associate with the human being. Scripture tells us that. Say's "seven eye's (this is the Bible), went out to disprove the human being as being worthy, and seven went out to prove the human being worthy".

So it's saying (that you have forces working to discredit your natural worth that G-d gave you, and forces working against that, countering that force, to prove you worthy). Now, in my opinion, it says, not just those who say, well, I'm not interested in religion, I won't bother with that, it's not that way anymore. It's also those who claim to have a sincere interest in religion, that's contributing to us seeing the human being in a different light, and not taking the human being serious as a creature of the highest plains in this material world, or among created things. Now, let's not think of ourselves as human beings in a world with white people. Now I know there might be a few white people in here; we won't hurt you with what I'm going to say here, my little experiment here. Now you're all black and pretend that no white people exist, and never ever existed.

For us in America, that means we don't have any literature. We never saw pens and a pencil, because it was of the white man that these things came into our possession after we were separated from Africa. Keep with the language. I said us, I didn't say Africans. Us, here in America. African Americans here, let us imagine that there are no white people. White people never existed. There are only the world, and animals. Plants and animals that's all we have. Now, in this world with no white man, no white folks and no advancement by them, we are looking at trees and the land in its natural order, untouched by man and looking at the animals and we're trying to figure out who we are. Who are we? We're not trees, we're not plants, we're not animals. We're not like the animals. We're different from all the other animals. How are we different from all the other animals? Now we're in this world and we don't have anybody to answer that question except ourselves.

Now how are we different from the dog? How are we different from the horse? How are we different from the birds? How are we different? Can we out run all of them? Can we out fight all of them, can we beat all of them, toe to toe, fist to fist? No! Do we have any superiority over them? If we do, what is it? Our minds, right! Our head, our thinking is superior to theirs! So our identity then should be above theirs shouldn't it? Our value, as flesh creatures is much above theirs.

155

I don't care if you give us the name humans, or in the Quran, Bashir. I don't care what name you give it, we're talking about that, that distinguish you from all other created things, and living creatures, that distinguish you from them, and put you much higher than them, puts you above them. That's what we're talking about. That's your true identity!

Your difference that stands out in creation, and puts you above all flesh as a creature that can do more with his life in this reality, than all other creatures. That's what puts you above all other creatures, and that's what establishes your individual, personal identity! We call it human, that's what we call it. G-d has made us human, and put us over all the other flesh that he created. We're human! So the white man come into the picture we're black! He didn't make us black, but he's white, so we have to distinguish between us and him. He's white, we're black. Are we going to take on a new name that we have to have to distinguish ourselves among white folks, and forget the first name that established our worth, our special worth, as creatures of G-d? Creatures created by G-d! You see how we have gone astray.

We have let the term, blacks become more important to us than our values. Highly valued, esteemed identity, thinking creature, planning creature, created creature, inventive creature. Allah-u-Akbar. That's our identity brothers and sisters, and that identity in its behavior that G-d created it to have, (in the behavior mode G-d gave it when he created it), it is the true Muslim.

Now, in the western society, we have seen human identity valued, promoted, defended, etc. There's not a nation on this planet, other than this nation, and the European nations, that this nation came from, that was made of, (their old citizens came here, and started a new nation, a new world) no other people have done more to promote human rights than these people. But if you understand the Quran, (and the Bible,) but I'm speaking of the Quran. The Quran is what awakened the west to respect the precious vessel, the highly esteemed creation, we call the human being. They were not always promoting human rights.

Before Islam came, they thought the common people were fated to be in the condition that they were in, and you should just leave them. G-d have intended for them to be like that. Just leave them alone. Women were not respected before the Quran came. There was no such thing as women's rights. No such thing as slave rights. Do you know that the Quran came and established slave's rights? The right to be free if you want to be free. That's one of the rights Islam established. The right for you to be free if you wanted to be free. And the right to have decent treatment whether you're a slave or free-man, to have decent treatment of a free-man. The masters, if he can clothe his children well; under the Prophet Mohammed ﷺ in Islam, at the time of the Prophet ﷺ, he had to clothe his slave well. If he could feed his children well, he had to feed his slaves well. The saying is, "clothe your servants or slaves, with the clothing that you wear, and feed them the food that you eat". I'm quoting our Prophet's instructions. Praise be to Allah.

So this was really awakened in the nations by the Quran and Mohammed ﷺ, this respect for the human vessel,

for the sacred human vessel. So we have this great
progress for the work force of common workers. This
great progress we have, because of the west. But when did
it start? It started with Quran, when the Muslims were on
the right track, and were sincere about obeying G-d and his
messenger. Yes! It started back there. Mohammed's ﷺ
community was the model of human excellence. Nobody
was treated like he was of an inferior stock, or an inferior
creation, no! The Prophet ﷺ wouldn't tolerate that. He
did not tolerate that. The Quran was against that.

In concluding this, G-d says, "my word is concluded, or
fulfilled in truth and justice". Everything is extended,
promoted, spread out in the context of mercy, knowledge,
(science and mercy). Knowledge or science, both, and
mercy. Those who gain high knowledge over others, others
are at their mercy. So this is a warning, an invitation, an
appeal, and invitation to those who will get that power
over the ignorant, and also learning if they understand it,
because G-d has done this. Meaning, if you go against this,
you're going to be overcome, because G-d is going to
prevail. G-d's plan, his will, his way. He and his word will

prevail. A warning to the nation, a warning to mankind.
Yes, you're going to come into great knowledge and
science, but be as G-d has been. He has extended it to you,
also with mercy. Isn't that wonderful. He has extended it
to you also with mercy.

Look how science has punished some of us. Look at how
science has punished some of our cities. Science, in the
wrong hands, or under the wrong authority. And look how
the learned have messed up the life of the ignorant. The
learned has messed up the life of the ignorant, have shown
no mercy. They have put us into a life that is nothing but a
constant struggle, can't take care of human needs, can't
have time with my wife, to have just a normal relation with
my wife and my children. I don't have the time. She's
driven, she has to work too. Both of us have to work. We
both are spending most of our life working, to pay bills,
and we're telling our children, "you stay in school, you
know if you fail, you're going to be on welfare, or in the
streets. If you want the good things that we have, you
better work." So can't you see that Satan has
accomplished what he said he wants to accomplish. He has
put us in a situation, where we're threatened by poverty to

the extent that our whole life is driven to have material things. Escape poverty, go to school so you won't be poor. Go to school so you'll be successful, and when you say that, you mean, you'll be able to get some money. You don't mean successful on judgment day, you don't mean that.

Mohammed's ﷺ saying, in the end of time (there will be many signs of the end of time) and one of them will be that the common laborer will be competing with the establishment to erect high buildings, skyscrapers. Mr. Johnson (of Jet and Ebony magazine), something in his soul, in his pride that G-d created him with, didn't like that all the buildings, tall buildings on the outer drive, were built by white folks. Mr. Johnson said "I'm going to put up one". He put up one. It's not as tall, it can't compete with those down a little further north, but you sure can see it from the outer drive. The Hon. Elijah Muhammad, he built the pioneers building, the office building, on the south side. He went up in the air. To us, it was a big thing. We've got architects, builders now; African American builders, who are building skyscrapers, building tall buildings. So the prophecy has come true. Here are the ex-slaves, the man that the world thought would never be able to do anything, would overcome slavery, the set-back of slavery, and be doing these things. Now he is competing with his master's children in building the world, the industrial world. And we're in there too, in that competition (collective purchasing conference). Our investors and our efforts. Our vision and our efforts. We're in there too, we're competing. Yes, and we're going up.

This day have already been prophesied of. Now, dear people, now that we see these signs. The signs of the end of time, you should see it as the conclusion of things, because G-d has said His word is concluded, fulfilled in truth and justice. You need the two. You can't have justice without truth, and if you got truth, truth says be just. They can't be separated, you have to have the two together, truth and justice. "His word shall be fulfilled in truth and justice." Truth against the lie of my worth as a human being. The lie that said I'm three-fifths of a person, and not a whole person. Three-fifths of a human being and not a whole human being. So that lie has to be defeated by truth if G-d's word is to be fulfilled, and his word never changes. It must be fulfilled. This is scripture.

All right, that's a lie, that my ability to handle my life, and manage this environment that G-d created me for, as he created white folks for, or anybody else for, is not as good as his. That lie has to be defeated. That lie has to be proved wrong. And there is something in our soul driving us, not all of us; it doesn't need all of us. You have more fingers than you have head's. You have ten fingers, you got one head. Four major limbs, one head. So we don't need all of us, we just need enough of us to be the head of this African American body, to revive this African American body with an appropriate head. That's all we need. So don't look for all of us to be on the same level. Don't look for all of us to be having the same drives. Never look for all of us to produce equally. Don't look for that. But look for the best of us to step forward so that the majority, (all of us) can have a better life.

G-d has made it that way, and that's the way it's going to stay forever. So we're living in the last day. We're talking about the last day for all of these thousands of years, and centuries now in America, talking about the last days, and the last days are here. I should say this, the progress that

G-d wants for us, is progress with our human life. G-d wants us to make progress with our human life, and make progress in every quarter of our human life. Not just progress for one part of the human life, and not the other. Progress for every quarter of our human life. G-d wants to see us make progress. Our progress with human life is our service to our G-d. You think Allah is sitting somewhere existing upon what we give him? He was existing before the world, and He didn't have a need for anything.

This is Islam, this is Quran. He was existing before the world, and He didn't have a need for anything. He created the world only for mankind, not for Him. He created all of this world for human kind. That's what He did it for. He doesn't need it, but He wanted of His own will and being, of His own existence. He had to create the world for human benefits, to benefit human beings, so that the human beings would experience the gifts of G-d, and qualify for even higher, more blessings to come. G-d had to do that, because his own being is loving, merciful, giving, kind, charitable, etc. He couldn't exist without giving. So He gave us the whole world, skies and earth. He has made for your use, for your benefits, whatever you see in the skies and whatever is in the earth. He needs nothing.

This is the Quran. G-d says, "I don't ask that you feed me." You need food, not G-d! He exist without anything, except His own being. He needs nothing else, so really, the progress with our Muslim life, is the progress with our human life in the state G-d wants it to be in. You hear what I'm saying? The progress with our Muslim life, is the progress with our human life in the state that G-d wants it in. Your true human life, before disobedience, is Muslim. So when we say Muslim in Islam, we're saying human in the best language of the civilized world. But there is another term. Mortal, (Bashir) for the human person isn't this wonderful that G-d says through Mohammed ﷺ? It's in the scripture, he's speaking through Mohammed ﷺ. He said to Mohammed ﷺ, "Say to them that you are a mortal like they are". "I am a mortal human person like you are". Now, this mortal human person is also in the right elevation for his growth in maturity and progress with his life.

This mortal human person is also the good news bringer. Think about this. Especially you deep thinkers, you philosophical thinkers. Think about this. Think about what G-d is saying in the Quran when he says that, "All of us are just mortals, human mortals". Mohammed ﷺ is one, and we are one just like he is, but if you are that special one, in the perfection of your human life, then you are also the (Bashirs). The good news bringers. And isn't that good news? I don't have to come out of my nature to bring good news to mankind. I just have to come into the excellence of my nature to do that. I don't have to come out of my nature to be a Muslim, I have to oblige my best nature to be a Muslim. I just have to satisfy my best nature, and I'm Muslim. Isn't that wonderful?

G-d did not give me a religion for something that's not human. G-d gave me a manual for human life. So G-d didn't give me anything foreign to my human existence. G-d gave me that, that my human existence was created to ask for. Isn't that something! G-d gave me something human when he gave me this Quran. He gave me my humanity when he gave me this Quran, and I didn't become Muslim in 1933, I was created a Muslim. Isn't that wonderful! And I was not just put on the path of G-d, with the coming of the name, Islam. I was on the path of G-d, when G-d made me want to see my humanity rise! I was on the path of G-d when I wanted to see my humanity rise, because to advance your humanity in accord with G-d's will for it, it's (siratal mustaqeem). Hey, you may not know it, but I'm responding to the book. It isn't coming from me buddy, I'm responding to the book, and to the model Mohammed the Prophet ﷺ, his (uswa).

All right, I think I've made my point. If you listen to the world tell you what Islam is, it becomes distasteful in your mouth. If you follow these dumb Imams, you'll get bored in your religion. If you follow the good common sense that I've given you today, you're going to get happier and happier, more energetic and more energetic, more creative and more creative, more industrial and more industrial, you're going to take your humanity further, because you'll know that you're really living the light of religion, and you're really living revelation, when you're advancing your own humanity.

But the religion is really nothing but an illumination of
your own original model that G-d gave you. It's an
illumination of that model. You couldn't illuminate it, just
like you couldn't create it. So G-d had to reveal to you that
illumination of your own human model that G-d made.
Now, I said it as plain as I wanted to say it. So I have a
spirit in me. I have a spirit in me that was with me before I
understood the Hon. Elijah Muhammad's teachings, when
I just heard the good stuff, responded to the good stuff, and
kept going forward with it, but not really understanding the
whole message, not really being able to carry the whole
message, to be truthful with you. No, I couldn't carry the
whole message. My own nature wouldn't let me carry the
whole message. I didn't fight it, but I didn't carry it.

What I mean by carrying it, I didn't put that burden upon
my mind to say I have to make sense of this. No, I said
"well I don't have to do anything with it. I'm just going to
take what I like and I am not going to touch that other
stuff". Yes, that was my position, and that was the
position of many of you under the Hon. Elijah
Muhammad. I knew it. We loved him so much we
wouldn't fight it. We just left it alone, and went with what

we could go with, and we sure could go with black man is better than the white man, and the black man should be saved and the white man should be destroyed. We sure went along with that. That was easy, especially those bad times we had back then. Bad times, and still haven't got it as good as we should have it. But it isn't left to the white world anymore, it's left up to us, and we're going to do the job!

So, in my conclusion, we are living in the time that has been predicted, the final days. We're living in that time right now. The signs are clear, big and clear, that this is the conclusion of things. The matter is being concluded. That struggle between truth and falsehood. That struggle between corruption and righteousness. That struggle between slavery and justice. Slavery and freedom. All that's being concluded now in this day and time and we don't have to be miserable anymore. We're free, and we have our provisions again. G-d says, "He gives every creature his provisions, from the heavens and from the earth", and another place he says, "He's given you provisions in four measures, in four measures." That means your natural life, your inherent worth, is the gift of

G-d to you. All of your excellence as a human being that's in your nature as G-d created it. G-d provided all that for you, and if you respect it, he will give you much more, as enlightenment, mercy, kindness, generosity. He just multiply his favors in your life. That's what he promised, that's what he's doing. He did it for others, and he's doing it for us. Yes! He's doing it for us!

So don't forget the human struggle. The human struggle puts us on the path of G-d, and we must continue the human struggle to stay on the path of G-d, and G-d will give us all the help we need to fulfill our lives in the most excellent way to make all the progress we want to make on this path. The Quran is enough for all humanity.

Mohammed the Prophet ﷺ, as a human model, to show us what G-d wants in us as human beings, he's enough for all humanity. G-d says, "He is enough for all humanity." That's what Allah says in the Quran.

You thought I said that didn't you? You should get more familiar with the Quran, and you will be able to follow me much better. I'm going to say that again. Especially you doubting Thomas's, [and by the way, I've got a neighbor here, the family name is Thomas. That has nothing to do with you. That's just an expression, doubting Thomas's], you doubting Thomas's - if you read the Quran and got more familiar with it, you would be able to follow me more smoothly. You wouldn't be snapping and carrying on. You would know what I'm saying, it's supported by the word of G-d in this great book, this book that's enough for all humanity.

So we thank G-d for this life and this time that we're in, and we pray that more of us become aware of the great signs of G-d in our day and time that are bigger miracle's and bigger signs of G-d's existence and his prevailing over all opposition than the separation of the waters in the day of Moses, and all the great miracles we read about (walking on water). What we see today is really more meaningful, in my opinion, more convincing, more relevant and more convincing than all of those great miracles we read about in scripture of old.

Those miracles, they can't be equal in value to the resurrection of the dead, and the advancement of human society. No! Those miracles, the best they did, was just strengthen the faith and kept the people going forward. But the real freedom and liberation, salvation, resurrection, progress, for human life, only comes with education. And that's what this book came into the world to do.

Properly educate the human family, so that we can have the great use of this wonderful creation that G-d created us for, and go forward with our human life, and know that going forward with our human life is really going forward on the path of G-d. Thank you. Peace be upon you.

So we ask G-d to forgive us our errors, our short comings. Forgive us our sins. Save us from the corruption of the world. Draw us nearer and nearer to yourself our lord, and closer and closer to the way of Mohammed the Prophet ﷺ so we will not be taken by the Satan. Ameen.

We praise and witness the existence of one G-d, and we salute the last Prophet with the traditional salute (peace be upon him).

In the conclusion of this address on this day, on the most precious day, the sacred day of ours, the Jumuah day, we ask G-d to save our lives, our hearts, from going astray, back into ignorance and corruption, after he have guided us alright. We ask G-d to give us in this life, good, and in the next, good, and to save us from the fires of sin, from the hell fires, Ameen.

We pray the prayer of Abraham, and the prayer for our Prophet Mohammed ﷺ. Oh Allah, make Mohammed ﷺ successful, and his followers successful, as You made Abraham successful, and his followers successful, and bless Mohammed ﷺ and his followers, as You blessed Abraham and the followers of Abraham; surely You are praised and magnified. Ameen.

ABOUT THE AUTHOR

Imam W. Deen Mohammed was unanimously elected as leader of his community after the passing of his father in 1975; the Hon. Elijah Muhammad, founder, leader, and builder of the Nation of Islam.

At a very early age, Imam Mohammed developed a keen scholastic interest in science, psychology and religion. He began his education, from elementary through secondary school, at the University of Islam in Chicago. Further educational pursuits took him to Wilson Junior College, where he concentrated on microbiology and to the Loop Junior College where he studied English, history, and the social sciences. However, his primary education has come from, and through, his continued pursuit of religion and social truths.

Imam Mohammed's astute leadership, profound social commentary on major issues, piercing scriptural insight into the Torah, Bible and Qur'an, and his unique ability to apply scriptural interpretation to social issues have brought him numerous awards and high honors. He is a man of vision who has performed many historical 'firsts'.

- In 1992, he delivered the first invocation in the U.S. senate to be given by a Muslim.

- In 1993 he gave an Islamic prayer at President William Jefferson Clinton's first inaugural interfaith prayer service, and again in 1997 at President Clinton's second inaugural interfaith prayer service.

- His strong interest in interfaith dialogue led him to address the Muslim-Jewish conference on March 6, 1995, with leaders of Islam and reform Judaism in Glencoe, IL.

- In October of 1996, Imam Mohammed met Pope John Paul, II, at the Vatican, at the invitation of Archbishop William Cardinal Keeler and the Focolare Movement. He met with the Pope again, on October 28, 1999, on the "Eve of the New Millennium" in St. Peter's basilica with many other world-religious leaders.

- In 1997, the Focolare Movement presented him with the "Luminosa Award", for promoting interfaith dialogue, peace, and understanding in the U.S.

- In 1999, Imam Mohammed served on the advisory panel for Religious Freedom Abroad, formed by Secretary of State Madeline Albright. He assisted in promoting religious freedom in the United States and abroad.

- In April, 2005, Imam Mohammed participated in a program that featured, "a conversation with Imam W. Deen Mohammed and Cardinal George of the Catholic Archdiocese."

There are many more accolades, achievements and accomplishments made by Imam W. Deen Mohammed. His honorary Doctorates, Mayoral, and Gubernatorial Proclamations give testament to his recognized voice, and the benefit of his leadership to Muslims and non-Muslims alike. He was appointed to the World Supreme Council of Mosques because of the value of his work and leadership in America.

Today, the dignity and world recognition Imam Mohammed has generated is seen all across the world.

MORE TITLES
Contact WDM Publications for availability

- The Story Of Joseph

- And Follow The Best Thereof

- It's Time We Sing A New Song [75 Select Poems]

- Wake Up To Human Life

- Islam The Religion Of Peace

- As The Light Shineth From The East

- Life The Final Battlefield

- Message Of Concern [Removal Of All Images That

  Attempt To Portray Divine]

TITLES
Currently out of print

- The Teachings of W. D. Muhammad (1975)

- The Lectures of Emam W. D. Muhammad (1976)

- Book of Muslim Names

- The Man and the Woman in Islam

- Prayer and Al-Islam

- Religion on the Line

- Imam W. Deen Muhammad Speaks from Harlem, N.Y.

  Book 1

- Imam W. Deen Muhammad speaks from Harlem, N.Y.: Challenges That Face Man Today Book 2

- Meeting The Challenge: Halal Foods for Our Everyday Needs

- An African American Genesis

- Focus on Al-Islam: Interviews with Imam W. Deen Mohammed

- Al-Islam: Unity, and Leadership

- Worst Oppression Is False Worship "The Key Is Tauheed-Oneness of Allah

- Growth for a Model Community in America

- Islam's Climate for Business Success

- Mohammed Speaks

- Blessed Ramadan - The Fast of Ramadan

- Plans for a Better Future: Peace, Inclusion and International Brotherhood

- The Schemes Of Satan the Enemy of Man

- The Champion We Have In Common: The Dynamic African American Soul

- A Time for Greater Communities Vol. 1-4

- Securing our Share of Freedom

- Return to Innocence: Transitioning of the Nation of Islam